Jesus

MAN, MYSTIC, MESSIAH

by

Hugh J. Schonfield

OPEN GATE PRESS
incorporating Centaur Press
LONDON

First published in 2004 by Open Gate Press
51 Achilles Road, London NW6 1DZ

British Library Cataloguing-in-Publication Programme
A catalogue record for this book is available from the British Library.

ISBN 1 871871 37 9

Cover illustration: *Christ teaching in the Temple* (1658)
by Gerbrand van den Eeckhout.
Photograph courtesy of the National Gallery of Ireland.

Inside illustration: *The Twelve-year-old Jesus in the Temple among the Scribes*
(1879)
by Max Liebermann.
Hamburger Kunsthalle / bpk, Berlin.
© DACS 2004

Printed and bound in Great Britain by
Antony Rowe Limited, Chippenham, Wiltshire

Contents

PALESTINE in the time of JESUS CHRIST

The Great Sea

PHOENICIA · SYRIA

Sidon
Sarepta
Tyre
Ptolemais
Bethsaida
Capernaum
Chorazin
GALILEE
Magdala
Sepphoris
Tiberias
Cana
Nazareth
Nain
Caesarea
Scythopolis
SAMARIA
Aenon
Samaria
Shechem
Salim
Antipatris
Apollonia
Joppa
Lydda
Ephraim
Nicopolis
Jericho
Jamnia
Emmaus
Azotus
JERUSALEM
Ascalon
Bethlehem
Gaza
Hebron
Herodium
Engedi
Masada
Beersheba

ABILENE
Damascus
Caesarea Philippi
ITUREA
Raphana
TRACHONITIS
Bethsaida-Julias
SEA of GALILEE
Hippos
Canatha
AURANITIS
Gadara
DECAPOLIS
Pella
Dium
Gerasa
PEREA
Philadelphia
Bethany-beyond-Jordan
Machaerus

Jordan

DEAD SEA

JUDEA
IDUMEA
Plain of Sharon

GAULANITIS · BATANEA

J.F.H.

0   25   Miles   50   75

Tetrarchy of Philip

Tetrarchy of Herod Antipas

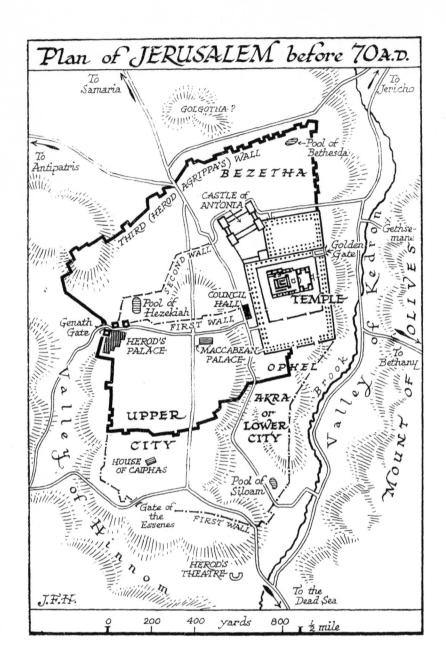

Plan of JERUSALEM before 70 A.D.

To Samaria

To Jericho

GOLGOTHA?

THIRD (HEROD AGRIPPA'S) WALL

Pool of Bethesda

To Antipatris

BEZETHA

CASTLE of ANTONIA

Golden Gate

Gethsemane

SECOND WALL

Pool of Hezekiah

COUNCIL HALL

TEMPLE

FIRST WALL

Genath Gate

HEROD'S PALACE

MACCABEAN PALACE

OPHEL

Brook

To Bethany

UPPER CITY

AKRA or LOWER CITY

HOUSE OF CAIPHAS

Pool of Siloam

Gate of the Essenes

FIRST WALL

J.F.H.

HEROD'S THEATRE

To the Dead Sea

Valley of Hinnom

Valley of Kedron

Mount of Olives

| 0 | 200 | 400 | yards | 800 | ½ mile |

Axiom

The teaching about Jesus was developed in three successive stages:

(1) the teaching about him by Jews to Jews,
(2) the teaching about him by Jews to Gentiles; and
(3) the teaching about him by Gentiles to Gentiles.

The Twelve-year-old Jesus in the Temple among the Scribes (1879)
by Max Liebermann (1847-1935)

Introduction

As I prepare this book for publication, with my eighty-sixth birthday behind me, I am very conscious of the long road I have travelled, and all the books I have written as milestones along it. Many of them relate to an obsession of mine, in time past an unusual one for a Jew, to comprehend the person of Jesus, especially in the character of Jewish Messiah. What Jesus was, and even whether he existed, is again being hotly and publicly debated as I write, and of course I have been caught up in this controversy. Unfortunately, it seems to be extremely difficult for those involved to transfer themselves to the time and country of Jesus and to experience the impact of the contemporary Last Times convictions. Instead they plunge into theology, or consider him as a sage, or as the central figure in a miracle play. Anything but adapt to *his* conscious concerns.

I do understand the difficulties, and it is for this reason that I have written this book, and also recount in it certain of my personal experiences. Let me then here introduce my theme.

Because of one man the name Jesus, a common one in his own time and among his own people as a Greek version of Joshua, has become a sacred one for many millions. Exalted to deity nearly nineteen centuries ago, he has remained for his worshippers an adored God-man combination with whom they have a love relationship because he is responsible for their salvation. Yet historically this Jesus was a Jew, who would have repudiated as blasphemy the notion that he was part of the Godhead. Is the transformation explicable? Certainly it is, if we can release ourselves from dogmas and examine the evidence dispassionately.

To make contact with the real Jesus one has to be objectively informed how Christianity as a religion came into existence. This involves not only the study of Christian records down to the fourth century AD, but also the social and political circumstances in the

1

Roman Empire in the same period, and in all its regional diversities. As it happens, this has become much more practicable by reason of the recovery in part or in substance of lost and unknown written sources, and the great progress of archaeological discovery. The Near East of the period with which we are dealing has been so reanimated that we can know its concerns quite intimately, and are thus in a much better position to evaluate the influences which affected the people of those times.

Among these people the Jews stood out, both among themselves and for others, as a strange and even mysterious phenomenon. They were a part of humanity and yet set apart from humanity. There were the Jews on one side, and all the rest of mankind (the Gentiles) on the other. This was seen to arise not only on grounds of religious beliefs, though these were very strong, but much more on function and destiny. Around the time of Jesus, in the Roman Empire, it had been written into the *Sibylline Oracles* about the Jews that they were 'a holy race of godfearing men', and again, 'the people of the great God... they who are to be the guides of life to all mankind.' Outsiders could not readily get to the heart of the Jewish phenomenon, and this was a cause of friction and dislike as well as of a somewhat superstitious awe. The attitude is still encountered today.

What had been at the nub of the matter can be expressed in one word, Messianism, which covers in the teaching of the Bible the means by which Man would be enabled to accomplish on Earth the purpose of his creation. In the vanguard of the fulfilment of that purpose would be a Chosen People as the Servant-Nation of mankind, which would only be able to succeed in its mission if it clearly understood it and was wholly dedicated to it. It was a task fraught with the greatest perils, not the least of which would arise from resentment at being required to be different, set apart from the pomp and pride of all other nations.

As an instrument of discipline, Israel received in the Torah (the Law) a kind of priestly code of conduct. When necessary, for correction, enemies of this people would be raised up to oppress and seek to destroy it; but also prophets and teachers to exhort and explain. Above all others a ruler would appear from this people, who by his example would demonstrate the qualities it must manifest, and who would be the means of its redemption. Thereafter, through the People of God, all the nations would come to know Him, and dwell together in peace and amity. But not before a final

2

manifestation of violent resistance by world forces to such an ideal state of affairs, which would deal a death blow to arrogance, domination and cruelty.

This Messianic concept, with some variations, was very positively to the fore among the Jewish people at the time Jesus was born, encouraged both by contemporary events and conditions and by the propaganda of Jewish schools of prophetic interpretation, which proclaimed the end of the existing world order and the advent of the Rule of God. It was a concept to which Jesus eagerly responded, being as he was a member of that family descended from the Jewish royal house from which the Messiah was expected, and by nature very sensitive to the Last Times atmosphere.

It is easier for me to understand this, because as a Jewish boy I was myself strongly drawn towards the Messianic, influenced by the apocalyptic atmosphere of the First World War. It was thus inevitable that I should encounter Jesus, and desire to get to know him and what he represented.

The quest has never been easy. There was much to unlearn as well as to learn, and one had to come to grips with the view of Jesus developed in Christianity as well as the wry sense of him in Jewish traditions, neither having much to commend it historically. Initially, I too was more conscious of the legendary figure than of the man who had given rise to it; and it required no small effort first to become familiar with the circumstances to which Jesus had responded, and then to see him in his assessment of them and in his dealings with them. Only slowly and progressively did there emerge an apprehension of the man's character and personality, thankfully extremely human and intelligible. This did not at all detract from his significance, but rather enhanced it. If ever there was a man with an exalted vision, with the skill and determination at all costs and with the highest altruism to bring it to pass, here was that man.

As this juncture it is needful to make some reference to my equipment. I could be said to have been fortunate in that I was a Classics scholar, a student of Greek and Latin, as well as through my religion familiar with Hebrew. My father used to make me and my elder brother translate from Hebrew into English three verses of the Bible before we went to school in the morning. I was also very keen on history and archaeology, especially of Bible lands. Thus it was practicable for me to conduct the researches which were essential to comprehend the Mediterranean world at the beginning of the

Christian Era, and to become well-acquainted progressively with the land and conditions which Jesus had known. I was able to develop this equipment with the help of great masters like Sir Flinders Petrie, Rendel Harris and Crawford Burkitt, and by a number of visits to the Holy Land and neighbouring countries. I was fortunate, also, in that many important discoveries were being made in Bible lands.

Moreover, I had the advantage of being, like Jesus, a Jew but not a rabbinist. That is to say, I was – so to speak – on the inside of Jewish ideology, having a native competence to comprehend and share a great many of his convictions and concerns. Also, as it happened, I was from childhood deeply drawn towards the Messianic, and by no means hidebound by tradition and religious orthodoxy. For this I should no doubt in large part thank my British background, and on the maternal side some inclination towards freethinking.

These statements may savour of arrogance, especially to Christian believers with their theistic interpretation of Jesus. But they are the simple facts. I have already made it evident that I hold such interpretation to have been wholly alien to Jesus himself. Therefore what I am saying has no motivation to put myself on a pedestal. It is intended to convey simply and directly that I could seek to reach out to Jesus more positively because of so much that was favourable to my endeavour.

I was to discover in Jesus someone who – to my way of thinking – knew much more than any individual I had come across what the Messianic was all about. He had come to this knowledge because he *had* to acquire it, as he became increasingly convinced that the rôle of Messiah was his destiny. Both the conviction, and the manner of his response to it, said much about him as a person, someone I very much wanted to know. He exercised an attraction that was irresistible, which transcended the academic and even the religious, once one had got over the hurdle of the misrepresentations of him by both Church and Synagogue. While he belonged to another age and environment, he spoke to me more perceptively about the meaning of my people's story than any other Jew of his own time or since. This circumstance already imposed upon me not merely a desire, but a determination, to discover and comprehend him.

Jesus became for me, as many would say, an obsession. I could see ever more clearly as the years passed that this had a significance which transcended personal satisfaction and enthusiasm for historical and biographical research. For nearly two thousand years Jesus had come to represent for Jews and Christians that which kept them fundamentally apart and at enmity with one another. This largely arose from ignorance and misunderstanding. Manifestly there was no hope for either while this state of affairs continued, no hope indeed for humanity at large until they were reconciled.

Therefore there had to be what would amount to a Second Advent of Jesus, which would disclose him in his real identity. It is significant that recently there have been both Jewish and non-Jewish scholars who have written about him more objectively as a human being. In the end this could be the only corrective of deep-seated errors, provided that it kept in view the self-recognition of Jesus that he was the Messiah. He must commend and justify himself by a more positive disclosure of his personality and ideology, which did not call for a theological interpretation of his status and mission, and which made it evident that he knew what he was after in a Messianic context. And in its true guise, what he had stood for had to be seen not only to make sense, but even to come as a revelation.

The impact would have to be such that it routed Christian idolatry and Jewish insularity, and opened the way for harmony to prevail between the People of God. That event would seem already to be long overdue, and further delay can only intensify the sufferings of the human race. But it cannot be pretended that the radical changes which are called for are as yet much in evidence, or that they can be accomplished without stubborn resistance and even active hostility. This, no doubt, is where the anti-Messianic (anti-Christ) will manifest itself, in a deceptive devotion to old-established creeds and religious institutions. One can see this already in the almost hysterical devout plaudits that have greeted the present Pope John Paul II in his pastoral tours abroad, and in the fanatical actions of Jewish religious extremists in Israel. The demand is still for Authority, which will take all responsibility on its own shoulders.

I have seen little evidence that the real Messianic is today anywhere understood or sought after. The whole structure of the modern world in a social, political and religious context, is remote from it. Of course there are many charitable and socially concerned people around; but the power complexes of our time have little in common with the Sermon on the Mount, and the remedies most prominently in evidence are predominantly authoritarian in concept and execution.

5

There is a cry for something salutary to manifest itself, and when it is not forthcoming there are pathetic demonstrations and protest marches. But the Messianic is not something that the powers-that-be of this world can formulate, much less create; and let no one who professes knowledge of Jesus exclude it. It represents an attitude to life that rests upon compassion and the rendering of self-denying service, to which it sees a whole nation, and ultimately the whole world, committing itself.

Very early in the proclamation of the Gospel – the Good News that the Messiah had appeared – the essential message was set aside, in spite of the preservation of a great deal that Jesus had taught. It was the significance of a Messiah that languished, more positively as converts from the Gentiles were involved. When Jesus was presented to them in Greek as '*the* Christ', by direct translation from the Hebrew for 'the Anointed One', the chosen of God, the Messianic significance was not adequately communicated. For Greek speakers the word 'Christ' did not convey anything commendable. Some accordingly preferred to speak of 'Chrestos' rather than 'Christos', a common Greek personal name meaning Good or Useful, which seemed quite appropriate.[1]

But it prevailed to drop the definite article and treat Christ as part of a name, or as a surname, Jesus Christ instead of Jesus *the* Christ, which suggested an inferior functionary. Thus the way was opened for Messiahship to be replaced by Deity, which was much more intelligible and acceptable for Gentiles of those days,[2] who were also familiar with double name gods and goddesses like Serapis (Osiris-Apis), Pallas Athene, Jupiter Pluvius, etc.

In previous books of mine[3] I have sought to make the circumstances clear to anyone willing to consider them objectively. In the following pages, however, I have largely sought to reflect the self-revelation of Jesus as disclosed progressively to my understanding. This called for a certain amount of autobiography on my part and some personal reminiscences, especially in the early chapters. Without these it might not be sufficiently evident how progressively I gained enlightenment. But I have had no aim to tell my own story beyond what was requisite, and I trust that my decision in this respect will not be taken amiss. Nevertheless, the book is a kind of *Pilgrim's Progress* of my investigations, with many of my publications serving as milestones.

I trust also that the reader will accept that I have not written this work with controversial intentions. Neither have I wished to give offence. But the times in which we live call for sincere effort in a spirit of goodwill to get to the roots of conflict and misunderstanding, and this can be a distressing process in some respects. I can say this without bitterness from personal experience.

Please try to come with me through these pages as a companion. It is possible that you may learn something I have missed, as well as what I have found.

Hugh J. Schonfield

NOTES AND REFERENCES

1. Suetonius, *Lives of the Caesars* (Claudius XXV), referring to Messianic disturbances among the Jews of Rome, describes them as 'instigated by Chrestus.' In *Philippians* i. 21 'Christ' has been used where the sense requires 'chrestos' – 'useful'. 'It is useful to me to live', not 'For me to live is Christ.'

2. See *Acts* xiv. 11-12, xiii. 21-22; *II. Thess.* ii. 3-4. Heathen kings were held to be divine incarnations. The Caesars were sons of Jupiter. See especially Suetonius, Gaius XXII and Domitian XIII.

3. See particularly *The Passover Plot, Those Incredible Christians*, and *The Pentecost Revolution* (in USA *The Jesus Party*). It also became essential for me to make a fresh translation of the Christian Scriptures (*The Authentic New Testament*, published by Dennis Dobson, 1955) with explanatory notes, because the translators of the Greek had not represented its actual literary structure and were not aware of many Jewish references and allusions affecting interpretation. Unfortunately, the *Authorised Version* of the New Testament contains some wilful mistranslations mainly for doctrinal reasons. For New Testament quotations throughout this book I have accordingly employed my own translation. I trust this will not be taken amiss. A revised and amended text of my translation with additional explanatory notes has replaced the initial one. It is available as *The Original New Testament* (Element Books). (For Schonfield's current publisher please contact Paterson Marsh Ltd., 11/12 Dover Street, London W1S 4LJ. [Ed.])

1.

I learn of Jesus

In my childhood Jesus was almost a total stranger to me. I knew virtually nothing about him beyond that he figured prominently in the Christian religion.

I had arrived in the world in London in the first year of the twentieth century in the very respectable Royal Borough of Kensington. My family could be said to be orthodox Jewish and orthodox British, highly patriotic in both contexts, and very middle class. I was not made conscious of any difficulty or strain in meeting the requirements of both allegiances. Indeed, in a curious way they seemed to blend. My mother came of a family which had reached England at the close of the reign of Good Queen Anne, and my father had received his commission as an officer in a Territorial Regiment at the close of the reign of Good Queen Victoria. Our domestic staff, nurse, cook and parlour-maid, was presumably Christian; but I do not recall that any of them ever mentioned Jesus to me. Neither do I remember that they ever went to church, though one or other of them may have done so.

At home it never seemed in those first impressionable years that there was any great distinction between Jew and Gentile. What was much more in evidence, was that we were a British household. The pictures on nursery and bedroom walls were chiefly of the royal family, and of the exploits of great generals such as Lords Roberts and Kitchener. My father annually attended the royal levies at Buckingham Palace in full uniform, and when gazetted major acquired a horse on which we children, and also my future beloved wife, were given rides.

However, despite my father's sturdy Jewish orthodoxy, Jesus in an unremarked way did get into our dining room. Adorning one wall

8

was a large canvas having as its theme *Peter denying Christ*. It was prized as a work of art, and its significance was never developed in conversation. But it did make some impact on me, enough to begin to speculate, and to be conscious of an alien religious environment surrounding the one to which I belonged. This consciousness was initially made concrete by a church, St. John's, at the corner of our road. I frequently saw the congregation coming out after Sunday service, and wondered in what way their worship differed from ours in the synagogue we attended on Sabbaths.

I had reached my first decade when the State religion came to the fore in a rather silly manner. My elder brother and I entered Colet Court, the preparatory for St. Paul's School, founded by Dean Colet in the sixteenth century. Our cap badge was a cross, and my father felt it undesirable that we should wear our school caps when we went to synagogue.

By this time I was becoming more curious as to what Christianity was about, especially when I was made aware that Jesus had been a Jew. The effigies of him that I saw did not look in the least Jewish. Why should a Jew be central in a Gentile religion?

From what I could gather from the Jewish side, Jesus had been one of a long series of failed Messiahs, the most reprehensible of them, since he had brought upon his people through the centuries untold suffering and persecution. Instead of being their deliverer he had become their foe. One of the first prizes I won at school was a history of the Crusades, in the course of which Christian fanatics had slaughtered thousands of unarmed Jewish men, women and children in Europe, before embarking for the Holy Land to recover the sepulchre of Jesus from the Saracens.

It was alleged by Christians, I was to understand, that Jesus had been killed by the Jews, and this was why his effigy was still exhibited in death, nailed to a wooden cross. The cross often had a notice fixed to it bearing the legend INRI, initials for the Latin words meaning 'Jesus of Nazareth, King of the Jews'. Poor king! Poor Jews!

Whatever had been the truth, a barrier had been built between Jews and Christians which has lasted down to the present day. In tolerant England it was almost imperceptible. At school the Jewish boys did not attend Christian morning prayers, but were not otherwise separate. All studied and played together, and became friends up to a point. It was not clear to us for the most part why it should be otherwise: religion was not a subject any of the boys thought of discussing.

Yet, however faintly, the uncomfortable distinction was there, and on rare occasions it could manifest itself at teacher level, because at St. Paul's School many of the masters were also Anglican clergy. It was one of these who in a very kindly manner, rather intending to be friendly, spoke to me of Jesus as 'our Saviour and your Messiah'. He was indicating what long after I was to discover was deep-seated in the Christian faith, that the Messiahship of Jesus was thought of as something significant for Jews, but of no special consequence for Christians, despite the fact that Christ in Greek was supposed to represent the Hebrew word Messiah.[1] For them it was Jesus as a saviour-deity that was paramount.

At that time it had not impressed itself on me that Christians worshipped Jesus as divine. The notion seemed so pagan. The whole business of Christianity was puzzling and intriguing. I had to know more. Particularly I had to know why Jesus was held to have been the Messiah.

From childhood the Messianic Hope had made a strong appeal to me, as it evidently did not among the Jewish boys with whom I was acquainted. So I was keen on the history of Israel as related in the Bible, and indeed on the history of the human race with which it was connected. I was thrilled to belong to a people whose mission it was to lead mankind to God, so that the world would become a place of peace and happiness. Only on occasions did I voice my interest at home, as it was ridiculed by my brothers. But I began to read voraciously about this planet's past, especially about the peoples whose story was particularly linked with that of Israel, the peoples of Egypt and Assyria. I delighted to view their relics in the British Museum, and I even essayed to master Egyptian hieroglyphics. Archaeology became my hobby.

The Messianic began to take an increasing hold upon my imagination, as something with which I would one day be involved in a positive manner. I have spoken elsewhere of my psychic experiences.[2]

My inward imaginings became intensified with the startling outbreak of the Great War of 1914–1918. No conflict on this scale had previously happened in the experience of mankind, a conflict waged by land, sea and air, and with new and horrible weapons of destruction. It seemed like a prophetic signal. Only weeks before hostilities began I had had my Barmitzvah (Confirmation): I was confirmed as a responsible member of the Jewish community in the synagogue, and read publicly part of the lesson from the Law and the lesson from the Prophets, invited so to do by my Hebrew name Joseph son of David.

I was now thirteen, a very impressionable age, and the war was one increasingly to stir the imagination. From the beginning it seemed something awesome, not wholly of this world. There was talk of Armageddon, of the Four Horsemen of the Apocalypse, of the Angels of Mons. The sense of participating in the climax of the Ages seized upon many, more especially with the start of the campaign to liberate the Holy Land from the Turks.

At this time the Jewish community became more corporately involved. My father was called upon for the recruitment and organization of the Jewish battalions[3] which fought in Palestine under General Allenby. The very name of this general, in sympathy with the spiritual concept of the hostilities, was arabized as Allah-Nebi (Prophet of God). My elder brother, who had joined up under age, was wounded on the road to Jerusalem.

It was at the West London headquarters for Jewish enlistment in Chenies Street (jokingly dubbed Sheeny[4] Street) that I met Zionist volunteers, some of whom had travelled from the United States. I was now sixteen. Among those who visited us was an ardent Jewish warrior Vladimir Jabotinsky, then a British sergeant, who impressed upon me that I must learn to speak Hebrew.

I caught the fire of revived Jewish nationhood, and decided to take up land work both to help Britain and to gain experience of farming with the object of settling in Palestine after the war. At the time I actually had a job as a junior clerk in a merchant's office in the City of London.

It so happened that I encountered a gentleman who belonged to the Christadelphians, a Christian sect very sympathetic to the Jews and enthusiastic on the subject of prophecy. We got talking, and he gave me some literature. So far as the war was concerned the Christadelphians were conscientious objectors, and many of their young men were on land work as an alternative to military service. Learning that I wished to take up farming, my acquaintance found me a job in a market garden at Feltham near London, where some of his sect had been taken on as labourers.

This was the first time I had ever been away from my family and in a wholly non-Jewish environment. I was given a humble but comfortable lodging with an elderly couple called Richards, who had a cottage not far from the farm. For me it was a stimulating adventure. Mostly I enjoyed cultivating vegetables, except in the depth of winter when it was very cold and bleak. An especial treat was to be chosen to load up and travel with the horse-drawn cart making its way through the night to reach Covent Garden market in the early hours of the morning with sacks of produce for the shops and hotels.

For George, the foreman on the farm, I was a phenomenon. He had never associated Jews with working with their hands as labourers, and could not understand why I should wish to do so. As a consequence he assigned to me initially some of the more exacting and unpleasant jobs. I don't think he had actually met a Jew before, and insisted that all Jews were bad. I told him, of course, that there were good and bad Jews just as there were good and bad Christians. He used to call me Alec, as I reminded him of someone of that name, and whenever a visitor came to the farm he would – if I was around – point me out to them with the chuckling comment, "Alec 'ere 'lows as 'ee's one of the good Jews."

With my Christadelphian fellow-labourers I got on very well, and they were keen to know more of Judaism. I was no less eager to learn what they believed about Christianity, though at this time I did not realise that their version of it was unorthodox and rather closer to Judaism.

I now borrowed from my lodging a copy of the Bible containing the New Testament, which I read for the first time. I found in it much to surprise me, and make me think. Here was not only a missing part of Jewish history, but a graphic account of Jesus in the capacity of Messiah. Here was, however, much else in these records, an evident antisemitism on the part of some of the writers, and the wholly repugnant notion – clearly alien to the mind of Jesus – which credited him with being divine. It seemed that converts from the Gentiles had taken Jesus over, reacting to him somewhat in the way that primitive peoples have frequently done when confronted with someone from a more sophisticated society, making him an object of worship.

These contrasts were very disturbing. I had not in those days the equipment to analyse the documents and investigate how they had come to be written. But I could judge that Jesus had not in fact been the alien personality the Church had depicted and led the Jews to believe from their experience at Christian hands. Jesus had been the victim of a ghastly misrepresentation, only excusable because it had not succeeded completely in destroying the reality. Here was a man

12

who seemed to have a great deal going for him in the character of
Messiah.

To say that I was moved and thrilled would most inadequately
represent my reactions. I discovered in myself that I was less of a
Zionist and much more of a Jewish Royalist.

NOTES AND REFERENCES

1. See above, p.6.
2. In my book *The Politics of God.*
3. Jewish wits gave them the regimental motto: 'No advance without secu-
    rity'.
4. Cockney for Jew, by reference to the glossy top hats normally worn in
    my youth by Jews when attending synagogue.

2.

I contact Christians

How did Christians react to the Messiahship of Jesus? What significance did it have for them? I did not go around asking such questions, at least initially. But I could gather from the views expressed by the Christadelphians and from my New Testament readings that the Messianic did constitute a vital concept in particular respects. The establishment of the Kingdom of God on Earth was the ultimate for Bible Christians, when Jesus would reign as God's representative. It was believed that after his crucifixion God had raised him from the dead and taken him to Heaven until the appointed time, when he would return to this world, overcome the forces of evil, restore the Jews to their land, and with his followers raised from the dead, he would reign over a peaceful and united mankind. The followers would include a multitude of non-Jews who through Jesus had effectively ceased to be Gentiles, and had become part of the People of God.

It was an impressive scenario, and went a long way to explain how Jesus the Jew had become central in the faith of Christians. There were alien elements in respect of the quality of Jesus, which cropped up harshly here and there. But on the whole adherence to Jesus did not seem to involve for Jews any change of religion, as it had done for heathen Gentiles.

I will come to these other elements shortly. But here I would like to emphasise how greatly attracted I was by the strength of the Messianic convictions I encountered. The great moment in Jewish history had come, and passed, but would be *coming again*. There was nothing in the hymns and prayers of the Synagogue which chimed so graphically with the emotions this aroused, the prophetic positiveness, the enthusiasm:

14

Now Zion's hill with glory crowned,
  Uplifts her head with joy once more;
And Zion's King, once scorned, disowned,
  Extends her rule from shore to shore.

    Sing, for the land her Lord regains!
    Sing, for the Son of David reigns!
    And living streams o'erflow her plains:
    What will it be when the King comes![1]

I was moved to the core of my being by the joyful assurance of such anticipations. I had not expected that I would encounter in a Gentile context such Messianic exuberance which had conquered the centuries and was eagerly anticipating a crowning fulfilment.

Apart from the Christadelphians, the Christians with whom I chiefly made contact were Tin Chapel types, simple, enthusiastic, evangelical. In many ways I felt closer to them than to my Jewish co-religionists, not in worship but in the sense of being caught up in the climax of the human story. I had never had any association with Rabbinical Judaism, which no more reflected the Old Testament than Roman Catholicism reflected the Jew. It may be thought that was rather brash; but I was still in my teens, devout and deeply affected by the developments of the last stages of the Great War.

What I was not in quest of was any other religion. As a child I had had a strong spiritual consciousness, and felt it natural to draw near to God in love and worship. Therefore, while I was delighted with the fellowship I encountered in the domain of the Messianic, and desired to learn much more of Jesus as ultimate Jewish king, it never suggested itself to me that I should attend services in Anglican or Roman churches. They represented, so far as I could judge, the more heathen face of Christianity, of which I had now become partly aware from the New Testament on which the Chapel folk relied.

I was beginning to appreciate that with the Christians the figure of Jesus had come to represent God. They did not really know or love, or actually need, the One they called Father. They were aware of Him only to the extent that they felt Him to be reflected in Jesus. God was Father because Jesus had related himself to Him as Son, and it was actually Jesus whom they wished to contact. It was he who had loved them and laid down his life for them, and as divine had resumed life like some heathen deities of old. 'I am the First and the Last,

15

and the Living One. I was dead, but now I am alive for evermore' (*Rev.* i. 17-18). I frequently heard the confusion of prayers addressed to Jesus, which terminated with 'for Jesus's sake' or 'for Christ's sake'.

The atmosphere of the *Gospel of John* was as strongly present in the twentieth century as it had been at the end of the first century of the Christian Era. According to that Gospel Jesus had told the Jews at Jerusalem, 'I and the Father are one.' The Jews justifiably accuse him of blasphemy, because being a man he made himself God (*John* x. 24-38). The author of this Gospel does not even allow Jesus the grace of saying, 'My Father and I'. The Jesus of this Gospel is in many passages thoroughly pagan, a nature god of the type traditional in Syria and Asia Minor where it was composed. His death is a divine sacrifice. But had Jesus really spoken like this?

One had to recognise the strength of the Gentile inheritance of Deity with a human face, which conferred on the worshipper a sense of comfort by reason of attributes akin to his own nature. Thus, to the contrary, man's demons were as weirdly unlike as he could conceive. Israel of old had been admonished: 'Thou shalt have no other gods before Me. Thou shalt not make unto thee any graven image, or any likeness of what is in heaven above, or that is in the earth beneath, or that is in the waters under the earth. Thou shalt not bow down thyself to them, nor serve them' (*Exod.* xx. 3-5). Yet the people turned to the worship of a golden calf, and delighted in the sexual service of the deities of the peoples they encountered.

There was always a deep-seated sensuality in paganism which was extremely appealing and enticing. Gentile Christianity readily took to it in a Christian guise in substitution for 'the Way of the Law.' This comes out again and again in the epistles of Paul, whose Jewish soul was shocked by the proneness of his heathen converts to immorality.

The Christianity I was in contact with was still pagan at heart, and its attitude to Jesus was still strongly physical, delighting in a sensual apprehension of the Messiah, even if this – at least on the surface – had been sublimated.

There were beautiful hymns that were sung at meetings, and the burden of many of them was of a human love relationship between the believer and Jesus. One of them was Charles Wesley's 'Jesu, Lover of my Soul'. But this was mild compared with other hymns. I may quote from two of them.

Still, still with Thee, when purple morning breaketh,
  When the bird waketh, and the shadows flee;
Fairer than morning, lovelier than daylight,
  Dawns the sweet consciousness, I am with Thee.

As in the dawning, o'er the waveless ocean,
  The image of the morning star doth rest,
So in this stillness, Thou beholdest only
  Thine image in the waters of my breast.[2]

Loved with everlasting love;
  Led by grace that love to know;
Spirit breathing from above,
  Thou hast taught me it is so!
Oh this full and perfect peace!
  Oh this transport all divine!
In a love which cannot cease,
  I am His, and He is mine.

Heaven above is softer blue,
  Earth around is sweeter green!
Something lives in every hue
  Christless eyes have never seen:
Birds with gladder songs o'erflow,
  Flow'rs with deeper beauties shine,
Since I know, as *now* I know,
  I am His, and He is mine.

Things that once were wild alarms
  Cannot now disturb my rest;
Closed in everlasting arms,
  Pillowed on the loving breast.
Oh to lie for ever here,
  Doubt and care and self resign,
While he whispers in my ear –
  I am His, and He is mine.[3]

Such hymns were sung in simplicity and largely in innocence; but they reflected an antique Nature-Faith which very early, as I was to discover, had coloured the Gentilised expression of Christianity. This is emphatic in the *Gospel of John* where Jesus is made to declare: 'Whoever chews my flesh and drinks my blood will have Eternal Life.' (*John* vi. 54)

There had become fused with the Messianic an inheritance from the worship which Frazer had described in his work *Adonis, Attis, Osiris*.[4] But in Christianity there had been developed a sense of immediate personal indebtedness. Jesus had suffered a tortured death for *my* sake, to rescue *me* from the hell to which *my* sins had condemned me. How could I do other than give him *my* love and devotion, the passionate and at the same time mystical sense of *my* gratitude?

I could begin to understand as I attended chapel and later on revivalist meetings the paramount position of Jesus in the capacity of 'saviour', the one 'who loved me, and gave himself for me'. But I, personally, found this concept alien and even repugnant. Orthodox Judaism had placed its own emphasis on Sin, and annually fasted and prayed for forgiveness on the Day of Atonement. This did not have a great appeal to me either. I could appreciate that it was needful to distinguish between right and wrong, and aim at doing what one believed to be right. But the term Sin seemed to give an almost grotesque magnitude to a great deal of behaviour which was of very moderate turpitude or readily excusable when one knew the circumstances.

My sense of God conferred upon me responsibility to determine for myself what I would regard as good or evil. The worst evils, for me, were those which wilfully inflicted injury on someone else, and the best goods were those which gave help in need. But in no way could I think of punishment as something meted out by God beyond the grave, when all the circumstances had ceased to be relevant. So where was there requirement for a saviour to excuse me from penalties which could never befall me in an after-life? Of course one should repent of doing what one was conscious was wrong and seek to make amends. But this was very different from passing over one's guilt to an innocent sin-bearer whose suffering God was prepared to accept as a substitute. It was this antique idea of a God who has to be propitiated and appeased that I found unwholesome.

This being said, there was evidently at the core of Christianity the personality and convictions of a man who sought to embody the Hope of Israel. It was this man I felt that I had to discover and contact.

Reading the New Testament had given me a novel and enormously exciting experience. It had disclosed and also concealed a moment in Jewish history when the Messianic had uniquely manifested itself. Nothing like it had happened among the Jews either before or since.[5] Inherent in it there was a sense of prophetic fulfilment, of a divine imperative, that was extraordinarily positive. One knew that either then or never the Messiah had to appear. The conditions could never again be so comprehensively appropriate.

Here was depicted the Just King, born of the line of David in the Land of Israel. In appropriate legend he had been the subject of angelic announcements. And, most convincingly, he had been no warrior, but rather the demonstrator of a sane and salutary policy for Israel, so that she should recover her ordained function in the world. This Jew had loved his people, and their welfare was so deeply upon his heart that he must reach out to them at all costs, especially to the desperate and the wayward, the sick and the suffering.

I was still a teenager when I was captivated and allured by the personality of Jesus. This man certainly had everything going for him as Messiah. No one had persuaded me, to bring me to this conclusion, no one other than Jesus himself. Yes, of course, I had the enthusiasm and the hero-worshipping propensity of youth. My critical faculties had yet to develop, and I had made no objective study in depth of the New Testament period and its literature. My response at the time was substantially an emotional one, to which the events of the Great War of 1914–18 had contributed.

But from the beginning I did perceive the distinction between Jesus as Jewish Messiah and the central figure of Christian religious doctrine. The allegiance I felt was solely to the former.

NOTES AND REFERENCES

1. From the hymn *When the King Comes!* by E. S. Elliot.
2. *Still, still with Thee* by Harriet Beecher Stowe.
3. *I am His, and He is Mine* by Rev. Wade Robinson.
4. Sir James George Frazer: *The Illustrated GOLDEN BOUGH* (Macmillan, 1978, an abridgment from 13 vols). *Adonis, Attis, Osiris* (IV/I).
5. The last claimant to be the Messiah to excite Jewish enthusiasm was Saboathai Zevi in the seventeenth century.

3.

Wanderings in a Wilderness

To get to know the real Jesus now became one of the great aims of my life. I felt that if I could do so I would be able to grasp the significance of the human story in its relationship to the Plan of Creation, and more particularly with that Plan to the function of a Chosen People.

Initially I had expected that I might learn much from Christian sources, both by study and contact, but here I experienced much disappointment as regards contemporary Christian doctrinal positions. I did go back to school, a Bible school, ending up at the University of Glasgow, where among other subjects I read metaphysics. At the same time I devoured Christian literature voraciously, and haunted the theology departments of second-hand bookshops. I discovered the Ante-Nicene Christian Library published by T. & T. Clark of Edinburgh, containing translations of the writings of the Church Fathers down to AD 325. I also read profitably various interpretations of the life of Christ, such as Farrar, Edersheim and Renan, and of course Schweitzer's *Quest of the Historical Jesus*. A great revelation was the contents of the Jewish pseudepigrapha of the immediate pre-Christian period, such as the books of *Enoch* and *Jubilees*, and the *Testaments of the XII Patriarchs*. The information I acquired was very exciting to me; but it would be boring for the reader to go into greater detail. I may mention, however, an incident which arose out of my pursuits.

While I was at university the Rev. Dr. R. H. Strachan of Edinburgh gave a lecture which had to do with the theme of the deity of Jesus. When question time came I had the temerity to get to my feet. I referred to the vision of Stephen in the *Acts of the Apostles* (ch. vii), where he saw Jesus standing at the right hand of God, and I asked, 'If Jesus was at the right hand of God, how could he be God?'

There was a titter from the students. I do not recall Dr. Strachan's reply; but when I saw him again in Edinburgh at his invitation, he charged me to pursue the Jewish origins of the Christian Faith. For my part I was very eager to comply, since I was now aware that within a quarter of a century of the death of Jesus there had been a rift between his Jewish followers in the Holy Land and his largely non-Jewish adherents in other parts of the Roman Empire. The gulf had widened rapidly due to a variety of causes – the different way of life of Jews and non-Jews, and the religious background of the non-Jews who became Christians which resulted in the creation of Christianity as a new religion.

But there had been other factors also, a developing antisemitism in many parts of the Roman Empire, of Hellenes against Hebrews, arising in no small part from civic and commercial rivalry, and the particular circumstances of the religio-political Jewish revolt against Roman imperialism which came to a head in AD 66, and caused the devastation of the Holy Land and the destruction of Jerusalem with its Temple to the God of Israel. As an outcome the Jewish followers of Jesus as Messiah in the Holy Land largely perished or became refugees in the East, including some of his own relations. Galilee, as Josephus related, was most severely devastated by the Roman forces, and among places wiped out in Judea were Lydda and Joppa, both mentioned in the *Acts of the Apostles*.

How in these circumstances could one get on the track of the Jesus of history? One could, of course, study and analyse the canonical Gospels. A great many scholars had been doing this very thing in the nineteenth century and the first decade of the twentieth. When and where had they been written and by whom? What sources, verbal or written, had the Gospel writers employed, and what were their personal motivations? Opinions often clashed. Evidently there was much to be said in favour of a special source other than *Mark*, used by *Matthew* and *Luke*, and which was no longer extant. It became known as 'Q' from the German *Quelle* [Source]. For the other questions there could be some clues furnished both by analysis and tradition. As regards the Gospel texts themselves these were very largely what had appeared in Greek, as represented by surviving manuscripts almost entirely from the fourth century.

There were advocates of a more primitive *Mark* (*Ur-Markus*) and attempts to determine which sayings of Jesus were associated with which incidents (*Sitz im Leben*). There were even those who considered that Jesus as an individual had never existed, and was the product of an artificially created myth. There are still some foolish advocates of this theory.

None of the four canonical Gospels as they stand was an original source in the sense that it gave reliable first-hand information entirely composed by one of the immediate twelve followers of Jesus. *Mark* comes off best in that it was prior to *Matthew* and *Luke* and utilised by them; and according to fairly early testimony its author had acted as Peter's interpreter, and had taken note of the things said and done by Jesus as cited by Peter in his addresses to Christian gatherings. Peter, of course, spoke in Aramaic, and in this Gospel some words of Jesus are quoted in this language.[1] The same tradition claims that it was not the intention of Mark to present all the circumstances in chronological order. It is to be remarked that Peter would appear not to have related anything about a miraculous birth of Jesus, and we do not know what – if anything – may have been set down by Mark about the circumstances of the resurrection of Jesus, since the text breaks off at *Mark* xvi. 8, and what is supplied from verses 9 to 20 is a later addition. In view of what we have noted of the Petrine tradition it is significant that in *Mark* uniquely the young man whom the women encounter at the tomb of Jesus tells them to go and 'tell his disciples, *and particularly Peter*, that he is preceding you to Galilee' (xvi. 7).

It is widely accepted that *Matthew* and *Luke* had some written sources at their command, and consequently neither of them can be very early. *Luke*, indeed, states positively in his Preface (*Luke* i. 1-2) that a number of authors of Gospels had preceded him. With *Matthew* the lapse of a fair amount of time is indicated by reference to circumstances which were still related (*Matt.* xxvii. 8, xxviii. 15). The origins of *Matthew* have been complicated by the belief which arose, due to a misunderstanding, that this Gospel had been originally written in Hebrew and afterwards translated into Greek. This was partly because early in the second century Papias of Hierapolis had composed a work in five books entitled *Logia Kuriaka Exegesis* [Exposition of the Oracles pertaining to the Lord]. In this he had said that 'Matthew composed the Oracles in the Hebrew language, and each one interpreted them as he could.'[2] The term Oracles related to the Old Testament, and it was attributed to Matthew that he had assembled in Hebrew those passages regarded as predictions of Jesus and fulfilled by him. We do find in *Matthew* a number of such

22

claimed fulfilments, which could have come from a translation of the Apostle's lost Hebrew work, thus linking the Gospel with him.[3] There were in the second century, as we shall see, certain Hebrew and Aramaic Gospels 'According to the Hebrews' and also a translation into Hebrew of the Greek *Matthew*, which tended to create some confusion.

We come now to the Fourth Gospel, which poses a problem even more complicated than that of *Matthew*, and which presents a very different image of Jesus to that of the other three versions of the Jesus story. Not only is this Gospel substantially at variance with the other three, it is quite different in style and in many details, crediting Jesus with extensive arguments with his opponents and hortatory addresses to his disciples. It is a theological Jesus who manifests himself in this material, bombastic, and in attack vindictive. Unlike the Jesus of the Synoptics he often speaks to Jews as if he was not himself a Jew.[4] The composition, to a substantial extent, follows a Greek literary style, where to sustain a prolonged discourse questions or comments, often unreal, are interjected at intervals.

Yet within this largely un-Jewish Gospel there are passages that exhibit an accurate knowledge of the Holy Land, especially of Jerusalem, as it was prior to the Jewish war with the Romans which broke out in AD 66. For example, at Jerusalem it is stated that 'there is a bathing pool by the Sheep Gate which in Hebrew goes by the name of Bethzatha. It has five porticoes' (*John* v. 2). In x. 22-23 there is reference to Jesus strolling in the Temple in Solomon's Portico during the Feast of Dedication (Chanukah) in winter time (i.e. December). This would be a natural statement for a pious Jew to make, but hardly for a Gentile, especially after the Temple was destroyed in AD 70.

We are confronted, therefore, in this Gospel with the work of two quite distinct writers which impinge on one another, the one a Jew and the other a Gentile.

To sort out this puzzle took many years of effort, as I shall need to relate in due course. The problem has been needlessly complicated by the supposition that this highly literary Gospel was composed by one of the twelve Apostles, John the son of Zebedee, one of the fisherman brothers, brash and impulsive, whom Jesus nicknamed *Boaneragsha* (Boanerges), the Boisterous Ones, 'Sons of the Wind'. Nothing could be more improbable. The other brother James, evidently living up to the family character, was later arrested and executed on the orders of King Agrippa (*Acts* xii. 2), apparently for treasonable agitation, since he was beheaded. Had John, the 'Dear Disciple', been one of the Twelve, his Gospel would hardly have required an endorsement of its veracity or an obscure reference to his identity.[5]

Clearly the Gospels held secrets which had to be cracked to a major extent before it could be practicable to apprehend the Jesus of history.

How, then, should I proceed? I was now engaged to be married to a childhood sweetheart, Hélène Cohn, and needed to earn a living to enable us to marry. My commercial capacities were minimal, and I would not make a good businessman. Neither was I very enthusiastic about any profession. For a time, with a younger brother, I acted as an agent for electrical goods, devoting my evenings to pursuing my studies. Since we lived at our parents' home we kept our heads above water; but very clearly there was no future in our enterprise.

Then something happened which transformed the situation. I was still haunting the second-hand bookshops in search of enlightenment. One day a bookseller opposite the British Museum phoned me that he had acquired an old Hebrew book which seemed to be in my line, and would I care to come and look at it? Of course I responded, and was startled to discover that the book was a printed text of the *Gospel of Matthew* in Hebrew, accompanied by a Latin translation, which had been published in Paris in 1555. Naturally, I bought it, though without awareness of the significance of what I had purchased. But there were tantalising title-pages at each end of the volume with Latin inscriptions. The one stated barely, 'The Gospel of Matthew faithfully rendered out of the Hebrew' (not, be it noted, *into* Hebrew). The other title-page more explicitly announced, 'The Gospel of Matthew, until this day laid up among the Jews and concealed in their closets, and now at last, from out of their apartments and from darkness, brought forth into the light.'

The work had a dedicatory epistle to Charles de Guise, Cardinal of Lorraine. This told how Jean du Tillet, Bishop of Brieux, while travelling in Italy in the year 1553, found the Hebrew manuscript among the Jews, and brought it back with him to Paris, where he commissioned a Hebrew scholar Jean Mercier, to translate it into Latin. Mercier, however, in his own preface is more explicit. He says that the Bishop had extorted the MS from the Jews of Rome for the purpose of examination.

When I could investigate the matter I was able to ascertain that on 12 August 1553, Pope Julius III had signed a decree for the suppression of the Jewish Talmud on the representation of the anti-semitic Pietro, Cardinal Caraffa, the Inquisitor-General, afterwards Pope Paul IV. This decree was carried into effect in Rome with great ruthlessness on Rosh Hashanna (Jewish New Year's Day), September 9, 1553. Not only had copies of the Talmud been seized, on the plea that it was inimical to Christianity, but every Hebrew book on which the minions of the Inquisition could lay their hands. It appeared highly probable that the Bishop of Brieux had found the Hebrew MS of Matthew's Gospel among the confiscated books. It was subsequently preserved in the Bibliothèque Nationale in Paris, catalogued under Hebrew MSS. No. 132.

I got down to reading the text with growing excitement, and in due course published an English translation with notes and comments (T. & T. Clark, Edinburgh, 1927). The document, of course, was not the assumed Hebrew original of the Greek *Matthew*; but it could well be a very early Hebrew version of the Greek and from a purer text than the great codices of the fourth century. *Matthew* in Hebrew had been known to the Jews almost certainly from the second century, and a copy was in the library of the Rabbinical College at Tiberias.[6] In the third century another copy was in the library at Caesarea assembled by the martyr Pamphilus, which was known to St. Jerome in the fourth century. He says that the Nazarenes (Judaeo-Christians) of Beroea (Aleppo) in Syria also had a MS of the Hebrew *Matthew*, which he was allowed to copy. This is of special interest since the du Tillet text has certain agreements with Jerome's Latin Vulgate, and he could have made use of it. He particularly mentions that in the Hebrew *Matthew*, as in du Tillet's text, the Old Testament quotations are from the Hebrew Bible, and not from the Greek Septuagint.[7]

As I got down to studying the text of my find I was thrilled to discover a number of places in which the Hebrew was better than the Greek and clarified the sense. In some cases words missing from the Greek were correctly restored. But there was something more. While the Gospel as a whole had not appeared first in Hebrew, the Greek author had access to and partly incorporated certain sources which were Hebraic. These included the Genealogy of Jesus and the section commonly called the Little Apocalypse (*Matt.* xxiv). There were passages which indicated the misreading of a Hebrew word.

Examples of what I discovered will be given in the next chapter for the information of the more erudite, as I will need to quote the actual Hebrew in some instances. But something of value may be gleaned by the general reader, who should specially observe the close likeness of certain letters which deceived the translator of the Hebrew source.

My life was to be changed in more ways than one by the 'miracle' that had happened. When the book was published it opened the way for me to meet great scholars in the field of Biblical research and Christian origins, among them Dr. F. Crawford Burkitt of Cambridge and Dr. J. Rendel Harris, who had specialised in Ancient Syriac documents.

I was also now able to get married, not because my book brought me some royalties, but because it got me a job with an advertising agency. A friend in the agency gave me an introduction, and a director having glanced at the book said they would take me on since evidently I could write and do research work. My first assignment was to publicise the potentialities of Malaysia.

NOTES AND REFERENCES

1.   *Boanerges* (iii. 17), *Talitha cumi* (v. 41), *Ephphatha* (vii. 34), *Eloi, Eloi, lama sabachthani* (xv. 34).
2.   Quoted by Eusebius, *Ecclesiastical History*, iii. 39.
3.   We are now much more familiar with this method of interpreting the Old Testament as prophetic of much later circumstances since the discovery of the Dead Sea Scrolls.
4.   Jesus addresses the Jews as aliens, i.e. 'you' and 'your law' (*John* vii-viii).
5.   *John* xxi. 24. (See also below, p.115).
6.   Epiphanius, *Against Heresies*, xxx. 3.
7.   Jerome, *Catal. Script. Eccl.*

4.

Nearer the Sources

There are passages in the Greek text of *Matthew* which convey that Jesus was a devout Jew, very close to the position of the Pharisees. One should ask, how could he be anything else if he claimed to be the Messiah of Israel? The saying in *Isaiah* ix, 'The government shall be upon his shoulder', was interpreted to mean, 'He has taken the Torah upon himself to keep it.' The predicted Jewish king must be a shining example of obedience to the Law given by God to Moses, so that his subjects would follow his lead. However unacceptable to a Gentile church, the representation of what had been the position of Jesus was too authoritative in the sources to be expunged.

> Let your light shine in the sight of men, so that they observe your good conduct and praise your heavenly Father. Do not imagine that I have come to abolish the Law and the Prophets: I have not come to abolish them but to give effect to them...
> So whoever would relax the most insignificant of command-ments, and teach men so, shall be treated as insignificant in the Kingdom of Heaven. But whoever both observes and teaches them shall be treated as of consequence in the Kingdom of Heaven. I tell you therefore, unless your devoutness exceeds that of the Scribes and Pharisees you will never enter the King-dom of Heaven. (*Matt.* v. 16-20)

These are strong words, and they are obviously from a Jewish source older than the Greek *Matthew* since they use Hebrew idiom. 'Our Father which art in heaven' is a frequent mode of address in Jewish prayer. The jot in the Greek text is the Hebrew *yod*, the tiniest letter of the Hebrew alphabet, while the tittle is the hook or flourish attaching to some other letters. When Jesus, in the full text,

27

employs these expressions, he is using an illustration which only has force in Hebrew or Aramaic to insist on the permanence even of the minutest precept. Similarly, the words 'Kingdom of Heaven' are those which a pious Jew would use when referring to the Kingdom of God, to assure that he was not profaning the Deity in speech. Other such indirect terms in use were the 'Name' or 'the Place', and of course Yahweh is converted into 'the Lord'.

Thus even in the Greek *Matthew* in many passages the Hebrew idiom retained in the text apprises us of an underlying Hebrew source, more emphatic in some cases than in others, where a poetic construction is involved, or a play on words. This is where the du Tillet Hebrew *Matthew* is so valuable: it enables us to perceive many things which otherwise we would have missed or not be conscious of. And in the process Jesus the Jew emerges much more positively, a man of his own time and people. It is for us to accomodate ourselves to him, and not, as in Christianity as a religion, to impose upon him a Gentilised personality with pagan overtones. Why does one never see a portrayal of Jesus that looks in the least Jewish?

Our first point of interest lies in the Genealogy of Jesus in *Matthew*. Evidently, for easy recollection, this was composed in mnemonic and didactic form, because the descent of Jesus from King David qualified him to be the Messiah. So the Genealogy was arranged in three sections, each listing fourteen names. In Hebrew the name David is composed of three letters (DVD) which have the numerical value of fourteen (4+6+4).

The Genealogy must therefore have first been compiled in Hebrew, and this was confirmed by the text I had found. If anyone troubles to count the names in the Greek text, as in our Bible, he will have found that the first two sections have fourteen names each while the third has only thirteen. Evidently by a copyist's error a name was dropped out. We would not know what this was but for the Hebrew manuscript. The missing name is that of Abner and follows Abiud (Abiur in the Old Syriac MS). Now in the Old Testament (*I. Sam.* xiv. 50–51) Abner is spelled Abiner. If the Hebrew original of the Genealogy read 'Abiud begat Abiner' (this would be אביוד הוליד את אבינר), the second name could be omitted accidentally as an imagined dittograph. In Hebrew MSS ד and ר were sometimes confused, and also ו and ן. The reader who has no Hebrew can readily recognise the likeness.

Another variant (*Matt.* i. 14) may also be explained on the basis

28

of a Hebrew source. The Greek has 'Sadoc begat Achim'. The Syriac reads Achin for Achim, but the Hebrew has Ammon. Again there is a likeness in Hebrew between Achin (אכין) and Ammon (אמון), which would be more pronounced in manuscript.

There are several other places where the difference between the Greek and the Hebrew suggests a misreading of the Hebrew by a Greek translator. I may instance a few. The Hebrew of *Matt.* xiv. 20 has, 'And there were left over unto them twelve baskets full of the fragments.' Here the Greek has, 'and they took up of the fragments that remained twelve baskets full.' Confusion appears to have arisen between ונשארו 'and there were left over' and ונשאו 'and they took up'. Similarly, in *Matt.* xvii. 12 (last clause) the Hebrew has יקבל 'receive', which the Greek translator has read as יסבל 'suffer'.

Among place names, for Gethsemane the Hebrew has *Ge-shemanim* as in *Isa.* xxviii. 1, where it is rendered 'the fat valley'. The reading of the Old Syriac *Gu-semani* points to the same derivation. *Golgotha* (*Matt.* xxvii. 33) is correctly given as *Golgoltha* in the Hebrew, and left untranslated since this was not necessary, while Arimathaea (*Matt.* xxvii. 57) is in the Hebrew *Ha-Ramathaim* (cf. *I. Sam.* i. 1).

One saying of Jesus (*Matt.* viii. 20) comes out more graphically in the Hebrew: 'The foxes have holes, and the birds of the heaven nests; but the Son of Man hath not a floor whereon he may lay his head.' The addition of the word קרקע 'floor', gives added pathos to this utterance, and could refer to accomodation in the khan or caravanserai of the village, where the rudest provision was made for the traveller in the allotment of a paved recess, raised about half a metre above the level of the yard where the cattle were tethered. According to Farrar, such travellers 'would neither expect nor require attendance, and would pay only the merest trifle for the advantage of shelter, safety, and a *floor* on which to lie.'[1]

In the Little Apocalypse (*Matt.* xxiv. 32) there is a clear case of a play on words which points directly to a Hebrew original. The word translated 'summer' in the Authorised Version is in the Hebrew text קיץ (qayitz) 'ripe fruit', while the 'it is near' of verse 33 refers to the 'End' verse 14, in Hebrew קץ (qetz). The same play on the two Hebrew words is found in *Amos* viii. 2: 'And He said, Amos, what seest thou? And I said, A basket of ripe fruit (קיץ). Then said the Lord unto me, The End (קץ) is come upon my people of Israel.'

Jesus quite naturally employed in his speech parallelisms as a form of emphasis common in Hebrew and often found in the Old Testament. Such parallelisms occur in the Sermon on the Mount, as for instance Mt. vii. 6, which may be restored to read:

Do not offer gems[2] to the dogs,
  or they may turn and rend you;
Nor strew your pearls before pigs,
  or they may trample them under foot.

We have another kind of parallelism in verses 13 and 14:

Wide is the gate and spacious the way
  that leads to Destruction.[3]
And many there are who enter by it.

But narrow is the gate and constricted the way
  that leads unto Life,
And few there are who find it.

At the beginning of ch. vii we have a further example, which has been lost in the Greek *Matthew* by omission and in *Luke* by expansion. The Hebrew has preserved the parallelism of the words of Jesus, and it is here followed by Jerome in his Latin Vulgate:

(A) Do not judge, and you will not be judged.
(B) Do not condemn, and you will not be condemned.
(A) For the judgment you pass will be passed on you.
(B) And the measure you use will be used for you.

Finally I may draw attention to the cry of Jesus from the cross. This is given in the Hebrew as:- אלי אלי למה שכחתני (My God, my God, why hast thou *forgotten* me?). This links *Psalm* xxii. 1 with *Psalm* xlii. 9, where the latter has 'I will say unto God my Rock, why hast Thou *forgotten* me?' Anyone may see how closely the subject-matter of the two psalms is related, and I will leave the reader to form his own judgment.

The glimpse I now had of a genuinely Hebraic tradition underlying the Gentile interpretations of the Greek Gospels was a great encouragement in reaching out to Jesus as he really was. The question now was, how much of the canonical Gospel accounts were dependable?

4. NEARER THE SOURCES

NOTES AND REFERENCES

1. Farrar, *Life of Christ*, p. 4.
2. In Hebrew the word in the source could mean 'sparkling things, gems', rather than 'holy things' (see *Lam.* iv. 1).
3. Heb. *Abaddon.*

5.

Facing the Facts

Looking back on the first decade of my quest I could say with confidence that I had had a rewarding glimpse of the man and the Jew that Jesus had been. This was encouraging. There could be no doubt in my mind that this individual had really existed, and was there for the finding. But how was he to be reached, almost in spite of the Gospels?

Initially, as I could see much later in my life, I had been too starry-eyed, too thrilled by the idealism of the Messianic, to be sufficiently analytical and objective. In this respect the fortuitous acquisition of an old Hebrew text of *Matthew* had been salutary: it had compelled me to study the Gospels more coolly and intently. I was a long way yet from competence to investigate adequately; but I could detect that the image of Jesus they presented had largely been overpainted and adapted, so that Jesus, like the Patriarch Joseph in Egypt, had become 'a stranger to his brethren'. The non-Jewish student would not be so acutely conscious of this transformation, since he would think it proper and appropriate that Jesus should be alienated from the Jews and from Judaism – not so much a gentle as a Gentile Jesus.

The great question was, how much of this Jesus was counterfeit, a wilful fabrication? Could the supposedly saintly men responsible for the Gospels, and indeed the early Christians in general, be imagined to be guilty of fraud and falsification?

I am afraid that here we are too controlled by standards of conscientiousness and the laws of copyright to accept as relating to the New Testament practices of misrepresentation in literary matters which were widespread in the period when the Gospels were composed. By many it could be thought laudable to attain believed good ends by the practice of forgery. It was also deemed legitimate biographically to adorn and amplify the account of one's hero by borrowing sayings and incidents from other sources. One could in those days invent speeches, which either had the aim of endorsing some political or doctrinal position, or less reprehensibly were deemed appropriate to the circumstances. The sentiments might even be alien to the views of the individual concerned, and would emphatically have been repudiated by him. The practice was common with the ancient writers of 'listening-in' to utterances and soliloquies of individuals, even when no other person had been present.

I was to discover that the New Testament was full of such inventions, worthy and unworthy, and even contained forged documents. But the facts were not faced up to because of belief in the Bible as the inspired Word of God. Among worthy inventions may be instanced the prayers of Jesus in the Garden of Gethsemane, where the nearest disciples were out of earshot and fast asleep.

As regards turpitude let the New Testament speak for itself. In the very last book of the Bible the author at its close puts a curse both on those who may seek to add to the text and those who may subtract from it. The author well knew that such wilful changes might be expected, and in this case the only persons interested in making them would be Christians. A century later than the *Revelation* we find Dionysius bishop of Corinth only too well aware of such practices when he declared:

> As the brethren desired me to write epistles, I did so, and these the apostles of the devil have filled with tares, exchanging some things and adding others, for whom there is a woe reserved. It is not, therefore, matter of wonder, if some have also attempted to adulterate the sacred writings of the Lord, since they have attempted the same thing in other works that are not to be compared to these.[1]

Since the majority of documents were written out by scribes and secretaries, and not by the author, and often copies were multiplied for circulation, forgery was more difficult to detect, especially in the case of alterations of genuine texts. The apostle Paul, whose work involved the writing and multiplication of letters, was himself the victim of bogus letters sent out in his name. He sought to meet the situation by signing every copy personally (*II. Thess*. iii. 17; *I. Cor.* xvi. 21).

To seek to separate the wheat from the tares was an arduous undertaking which could not be embarked upon without prolonged research. But I was now ready to make an initial excursion at one point, the contradictory accounts of the birth of Jesus given by *Matthew* and *Luke*. Clearly what was related was largely legend, designed to emphasise that Jesus had come into this world with all the heavenly endorsements of his Messianic status that were appropriate. If one did not assume that all the details were real events the device of legend was not illegitimate at a time when it was common practice to adorn the advents of significant individuals with supernatural embellishments. Among the Jews themselves there were current around the same period comparable legends of the birth of Abraham and Moses. There were like-ingredients, the tyrant king, the astrologers who determine from stars that a babe is to be born to effect a radical change, the attempt to destroy the child in infancy and his miraculous preservation. Why is this suppressed by the Church?

In respect of such legends there is less to quarrel with in *Matthew* than in *Luke*, since *Luke* professes to be recording history. He is ready to borrow from the past, notably from the Biblical account of the birth of the Prophet Samuel. But he has also another major purpose, to provide an effective challenge to the contemporary body of believers who endorsed the Messiahship of John the Baptist. The New Testament tells us that many Jews were wondering whether John the Baptist could be the Messiah, and even that he had a following. But it does not make clear, as other sources do, that there was a very substantial body of Jews who were convinced that John was the Messiah, rivalling the champions of Jesus and sometimes in controversial discussion with them. It is also suppressed in the New Testament that there was a contemporary belief, sponsored by the Essenes, that there would be two Messiahs, one priestly and one regal, respectively from the tribes of Levi and Judah. The early Christians favoured the view of the Pharisees, that rather than a Priestly Messiah there would be a priestly forerunner of the Royal Messiah, whom they identified with the reincarnation of the Prophet Elijah (*Malachi* iv. 5-6), whom they insisted had been a priest.

There was a pointer to the Christian concern that John the Baptist should be a rival to Jesus in several places in the Gospels. In the account of John's preaching, immediately before Jesus comes to be baptised, John announces that the one who is coming is mightier than himself. He is not worthy to carry, or untie, his shoes. John is not attacked. He is lauded as the forerunner; but he is emphatically put in a subordinate place. No one is greater than the Baptist, yet he that

34

is least in the Kingdom of Heaven is greater than he (*Matt*.xi.11, *Luke* vii. 28). In *John* the Baptist emphasises his inferiority and repudiates his Messiahship. The Baptist tells the Jews without the slightest hesitation, 'I am not the Messiah' (*John* i. 20, and see *John* iii. 28-30). This is blatant Christian propaganda fathered upon the Baptist.

I must confess that I had not contemplated in this early period of my quest that it would be greatly complicated by Christian misrepresentation. I had considered that there would be problems in getting behind the paganised presentation of Jesus in Christian teaching. But I had not reckoned with such extensive manipulation. My initial researches into the Nativity stories proved to be very beneficial: they were both enlightening and to a degree shocking. Some of my readers may be even more affected than I was, since they have been accustomed to treat the New Testament, and especially the Gospels, as 'Gospel Truth'.

It was speedily disclosed to me that the believers in the Messiahship of John the Baptist had had their own legends of his nativity and infancy, which the Christians had partially laid under tribute and to an extent appropriated in favour of Jesus. One of the hurdles to be overcome had been that John the Baptist would appear to have actually been born in the region of Bethlehem, while Jesus had been born in Galilee.

I could discern that behind the Gospel stories there must have been a lost *Book of the Nativity of John*,[2] which had been imitated and borrowed from. Thankfully it did not prove too difficult to ascertain that there had been a Baptist book of this nature, even if no copy was now available.

It may be asked why we should suppose that Christians would act in this way. The short answer is that we have proof that they could in that they employed the account of the birth of John the Baptist in *Luke* to compose a *Book of the Nativity of Mary* (the mother of Jesus). We find this in the apocryphal *Book of James* and the *Gospel of the Nativity of Mary*, both extant. The following comparisons will make the facts clear.

Nativity of Mary	Nativity of John
[Mary's] father was named Joachim, and her mother Anna... Their life was guileless and right before the Lord, and irreproachable and pious before men... For about twenty years they lived in their own house, a chaste married life, without	There was... a certain priest named Zacharias, of the course of Abia: and his wife was of the daughters of Aaron, and her name was Elizabeth. And they were both righteous before God, walking in all the commandments and ordinances

(Nativity of Mary)   (Nativity of John)

having any children (because Anna was barren). (*Nativity of Mary*, i)

of the Lord blameless. And they had no child, because that Elizabeth was barren, and they were both now well-stricken in years. (*Luke* i. 5-7)

Now... on a certain day when he [Joachim] was alone, an angel of the Lord stood by him in a great light. And when he was disturbed at his appearance, the angel who had appeared to him restrained his fear, saying: Fear not, Joachim, nor be disturbed by my appearance; for I am the angel of the Lord sent by Him to thee to tell thee that thy prayers have been heard, and that thy charitable deeds have gone up into His presence... Accordingly, thy wife, Anna, will bring forth a daughter to thee, and thou shalt call her name Mary: she shall be consecrated to the Lord from her infancy, and she shall be filled with the Holy Spirit, even from her mother's womb. She shall neither eat nor drink any unclean thing. (*Nativity of Mary*, iii)

And there appeared unto him [Zacharias] an angel of the Lord standing on the right side of the altar of incense. And when Zacharias saw him, he was troubled, and fear fell upon him. But the angel said unto him, Fear not, Zacharias; for thy prayer is heard and thy wife Elizabeth shall bear thee a son, and thou shalt call his name John. And thou shalt have joy and gladness; and many shall rejoice at his birth. For he shall be great in the sight of the Lord, and shall drink neither wine nor strong drink; and he shall be filled with the Holy Spirit, even from his mother's womb. (*Luke* i. 11-15)

And her months were fulfilled, and in the ninth month Anna brought forth [a daughter]... and on the eighth day she called her name Mary. (*Book of James* v)

Now Elizabeth's full time came that she should be delivered; and she brought forth a son... And it came to pass on the eighth day they came to circumcise the child; and they called him [John]. (*Luke* i. 57, 60)

And Anna made a song to the Lord God, saying: I will sing to the Lord my God, for he hath looked upon me, and hath taken away the reproach of mine enemies [etc.]. (*Book of James* vi)

And she[3] [i.e. Elizabeth] said, My soul doth magnify the Lord, and my spirit hath rejoiced in God my Saviour, for he hath regarded the disgrace of his handmaiden [etc.]. (*Luke* i. 46-48)

Then Anna, filled with the Holy Spirit, said before them all: The Lord Almighty, the God of Hosts, being mindful of his work, hath visited his people with a good and holy visitation, to bring down the hearts of the Gentiles who were rising against us. He hath opened his ears to our prayers: he hath kept away from us the exulting of all our enemies [etc.]. (*Pseudo-Matthew* v)

And his father Zacharias was filled with the Holy Spirit, and prophesied saying, Blessed be the Lord God of Israel; for he hath visited and redeemed his people... as he spake by the mouth of his holy prophets, which have been since the world began: that we should be saved from our enemies, and from the hand of all that hate us; [etc.]. (*Luke* i. 67-68, 70-71)

And the virgin of the Lord advanced in age and virtues. (*Nativity of Mary* vii)

And the child grew, and waxed strong in spirit. (*Luke* i. 80)

While the actual text of the *Book of the Nativity of John* has not
as yet been recovered there are a number of traditions going back to
the time of the Early Church which report elements of the legends in
which John the Baptist figures as the infant Messiah. These are mainly
found in the East in Syriac works, and in the *Book of John* of the
Mandaeans, the remnant of the sect in Iraq which endorsed John's
Messiahship. I was able to assemble this material in a monograph.

Whilst I cannot develop the theme here, I can give some indication
of its import in one or two quotations from the sources. I will take
first the *Commentaries on the Gospels* [4] of Isho'dad, a Nestorian
bishop of the ninth century. On *Matthew* iii.1, 'And in those days
came John the Baptist,' he reports as follows:

But how was John removed?

Mar Ephraim [Ephraim the Syrian, fourth century] and others say that
Elizabeth withdrew him from before the sword of Herod; she had
received in a revelation that she should make him flee to the wilderness...

Others say, that at one time, our Lord fled before the sword of
Herod, and so did His messenger... and the one [i.e. Jesus] rode on
an ass, but the other on the rush of the wind, like Habakkuk... (*Bel
and the Dragon*, xxxvi) [5]

Others say, that when Zachariah his father felt the sword of Herod,
perhaps the boy was sought; for he was from the border of Bethlehem,
although he dwelt in Jerusalem on account of the high priesthood [sic],
and he took the child and put him on the altar of propitiation, where
he had received the conception [annunciation?] by means of the angel.
While he was blessing about this in prayer, the angel seized him [i.e.
John] and took him away to the inner wilderness. But afterwards the
Jews inquired about his son, 'Where is the prophet that was born to
save Israel from the oppression of the Romans?' And he truthfully
replied, 'I do not know.' They answered him cruelly: 'Because thou
art envious about the liberation of the people, thou hast killed thy son,
in order that we may not be free from bondage' – for they expected a
Messiah from the wonders that were performed at his conception and
at his birth.

We are here apprised of a cycle of Baptist Nativity legends, with
which we make more direct contact in the Mandaean *Sidra d'Yahya* [*Book of John*], but in a much more exotic form. I will quote a
short passage: [6]

The Annunciation (Book of John, 18)

A child was planted out of the height, a mystery revealed in Jerusalem.
The priests saw dreams; chill seized on their children, chill seized on
Jerusalem.

(One of the priests relates to his fellows a vision he has seen.)
...I slept not and rested not, [and I beheld] that a star appeared and
stood over Enishbai [Elizabeth]. Fire burned in old father Zakhria [i.e.
he was filled with the spirit of prophecy]; three heaven-lights appeared
[cf. the three Magi]... A star flew down into Judea, a star flew down
into Jerusalem...

(The priests are dismayed at the vision, and the High Priest Eliezer is
advised to send to Lilyukh [Elijah?] for an interpretation. Lilyukh
interprets the vision and expounds it in a letter):
... Lilyukh writes unto them in the letter and says to them: The star
that came and stood over Enishbai: a child will be planted out of the
height from above: he comes and will be given to Enishbai. The fire
that burned in old father Zakhria: Yohana will be born in Jerusalem.

The birth and infancy of John are not recorded in this division,
which confines itself to the prophetic annunciation with incidental
details. In section 32, however, particulars of the nativity and the escape of John are related by himself, and these we shall now proceed
to quote in full:

My father, says Yahya, was ninety and nine and my mother eighty
and eight years old. Out of the basin of Jordan [the River of Life] they
[the angels] took me. They bore me up and laid me in the womb of
Enishbai. Nine months, said they, thou shalt stay in her womb, as do
all other children. No wise woman [midwife], said he, brought me into
the world in Judea... I was born from Enishbai in the region of Jerusalem.

The region of Jerusalem quakes and the wall of the priests rocks.
Elizar, the great house [the High Priest Eliezer?], stands there and his
body trembles. The Jews gather together, come unto old father Zakhria
and they speak to him: O old father Zakhria, thou art to have a son.
Tell us now, what name shall we give him? Shall we give him for name
'Yaqif of Wisdom', that he may teach the Book in Jerusalem? Or shall
we give him for name 'Zatan the Pillar', so that the Jews may swear
by him and commit no deceit?

When Enishbai heard this, she cried out and said: Of all these names
which you name will I not give him one; but the name Yahya-Yohana[7]
will I give him, [the name] which Life's self has given unto him.

38

When the Jews heard this, they were filled with wicked anger against her and said: What weapon shall we make ready for [a certain] one and his mother, that he be slain by our hand?

When Anosh, the treasure [the Son of Man?], heard this he took the child and brought it to Parwan, the white mountain, to Mount Parwan on which sucklings and little ones on holy drink are reared up.

[There I remained] until I was two and twenty years old. I learned there the whole of my wisdom and made fully my own the whole of my discourse. They clothed me with vestures of glory and veiled me with cloud-veils.

They wound round me a girdle, of [living] water a girdle, which shone beyond measure and glistened. They set me within a cloud, a cloud of splendour, and in the seventh hour of a Sunday they brought me to the Jerusalem region. Then cried a voice in Judea, a crying proclaimed in Jerusalem. They call out: What woman had a son, who then was stolen? What woman has made for him a vow and been heedless about it? What woman had a son, who was stolen? Let her come and see after her son.

Who told Battai, who instructed Battai, who told Battai to go and say to Enishbai: A youth has come to Judea, a prophet has come to Jerusalem. A youth has come to Judea: his guardian angel stands by him. His mouth is like thee and his lips [like] his father, old father Zakhria. His nose is like thee and his hands [like] his father, old father Zakhria.

When Enishbai heard this, she hurried out veil-less. When old father Zakhria saw her thus, he wrote her a bill of divorcement... The Sun opened his mouth and spake to old father Zakhria in Jerusalem: Old father Zakhria, thou great dotard[?], who has grown old and lost his wits... A youth has come to Judea; why dost thou send Enishbai away?

When the youth saw her alone, he set himself free and fell down from the cloud... and kissed the mouth of Enishbai. When Anosh, the treasure, saw him [do this], he spake unto Yahya in Jerusalem: Stands it for thee written in thy book, is it declared unto thee on thy page, to kiss her alone, on the mouth?' Thereon answered Yahya and spake unto Anosh, the treasure, in Jerusalem: Nine months I abode in her womb, so long as all other children abide there, without any reluctance on her part; therefore is it no charge against me now to kiss her alone, on the mouth. Nay, hail and again hail to the man who repays father and mother in full. A man who recompenses father and mother, has not the like in the world...

The most significant thing about these colourful Mandaean representations of the Messiahship of John the Baptist is that they favour the Essene doctrine of the Man (Son of Man)[8] and are in line with the tradition that the Messiah would be spirited away. As regards this tradition, the Jewish Midrash *Shir haShirim Rabba* on *Cant.* ii. 9, 'My beloved is like a roe or a young hart,' comments: 'A roe appears and is hid, appears and is hid again. So our first redeemer [Moses] appeared and was hid, and at length appeared again. So our last redeemer [the Messiah] shall be revealed to them, and shall be hid again from them... and shall be revealed again.'

In the *Jerusalem Talmud*[9] the story is told of the birth of the Messiah in Bethlehem. The news is given to a Jewish farmer by an Arabian. The farmer sells his oxen and plough and purchases infant garments which he takes to Bethlehem as merchandise. He finds the mother of the Messiah, who tells him she has no money to buy the clothes. He tells her to keep them and she can pay at a future time. When he returns, however, and inquires after the infant, she tells him, 'Since you saw me last, winds and tempests came and snatched him away out of my hands.'

The Arabian here takes the place of the Magi, in this case linked with the tradition behind the Baptist legend where the Messiah in infancy is spirited away to conceal him from his enemies. How well established this mythology was may be seen from its appropriation near the end of the first century AD by the author of the *Apocalypse of John* (*Rev.* xii), in this case in relation to the deliverance of the Jewish faithful from the might of Rome. I quote the first part of the vision:

> Now there appeared in heaven a great sign, a Woman clothed with the sun, with the moon beneath her feet, and upon her head a wreath of twelve stars. She was with child, and cried out in her pangs straining to be delivered. Another sign also appeared in heaven. This took the form of a great fiery Dragon with seven heads and ten horns, whose tail carried away a third of the stars of heaven and flung them to earth. The Dragon stood before the Woman who was about to give birth, so that when her child was born he could devour it. She bore a Son, a male child, who is to herd all nations with an iron-shod staff; but the child was snatched away to God and to his throne. The Woman fled to the wilderness, where she has a place prepared for her by God, for her to be cared for there for twelve hundred and sixty days. (*Rev.* xii. 1-6)[10]

Quite evidently there was much more behind the myths and legends than met the eye. And these represented only a fraction of the material that was going to require investigation, material that is never communicated to Christian congregations, or taught in Bible Class. But unless one was going to be thorough and open-minded, sympathetic and yet critical, ready to appreciate the influence both of adornment and falsification, there could be no prospect of getting anywhere near the reality.

NOTES AND REFERENCES

1. Eusebius, *Ecclesiastical History*, iv. 23.
2. This was the title of the book on this theme I published in 1929, namely *The Lost 'Book of the Nativity of John'* (T. & T. Clark, Edinburgh).
3. Church authorities attribute the *Magnificat* to Mary, but the text points to Elizabeth who had suffered the disgrace of being barren.
4. Translated from the Syriac by Dr. Margaret Gibson (CUP).
5. The rescue of the infant Messiah by air was a feature of one cycle of legends.
6. For the full English text see G. R. S. Mead, *The Gnostic John the Baptizer* (John M. Watkins, London, 1924).
7. Both names stand for John, but the first is the Arabic form while the second is Mandaean.
8. In the *Sidra d'Yahya* John the Baptist is actually referred to as 'The Man who is sent by the King' (i.e. God).
9. Tractate *Berachoth*, fol. 5, col. 1.
10. See *The Original New Testament* (tr. Schonfield), pp. 568ff.

6.

The Other End of the Story

The four canonical Gospels, substantially as we now know them, were in existence by the early part of the second century AD, that is, approximately one hundred years after the death of Jesus. The exact year of his death is, at this juncture, immaterial. What I have briefly illustrated is that within so short a period there had ceased to be any clear and wholly reliable record of when, where, and in what circumstances Jesus had come into this world. The information given is partly borrowed, partly contradictory, and substantially mythological. The period can be reduced still further, because for at least one third of that hundred years there could be expected to have survived some individuals, notably the younger members of the family to which Jesus belonged, capable of giving more detailed and exact information.[1]

I am, of course, restricting myself here to the records regarded by the Church as the most authoritative. It cannot be ruled out that there had existed older written sources, conceivably more dependable, to which we do not as yet have direct access. We also have to appreciate that the Jews were not greatly interested in biographical information in respect of their heroes prior to the time when they were called to embark on their particular function or ministry. This would help to explain our total lack of records of the activities of Jesus from childhood until the commencement of his ministry, a large slice of at least twenty years out of a short life. Additionally we must face the fact that between the life of Jesus and the composition of the Gospels lies the great war between the Jews and Romans which devastated both Galilee and Judea and was responsible for enormous loss of life. We know that even the personal recollections of many who survived were confused. And then there is the evidence that none of the canonical Gospels was written in the Holy Land or in Hebrew or Aramaic.

While also these considerations relate especially to the birth and youth of Jesus, how do they affect the other end of the story, his death and alleged resurrection? Here again when we examine the accounts we discover that they are largely fabricated and mythological, making it extremely difficult to extract very much of historical worth. There is also a strong element of apologetic as regards Rome and of antisemitic propaganda, especially in the later Gospels. The Roman governor is depicted as behaving not only in a manner contrary to his known character, as I shall demonstrate, but also in violation of his status as Rome's representative.

There was an early tradition that Matthew had set down a compendium of Old Testament passages held to be applicable to Jesus as Messiah. One section covered the circumstances of his death (see *Luke* xxiv. 26). This kind of interpretation was practised by the Essene holy men around the beginning of the Christian Era, as we have discovered since the Dead Sea Scrolls came to light. Prophetic texts were given supposed fulfilments. And this, it would seem, was what happened in respect of the trial and execution of Jesus, at least as regards major elements suggested, for example, by *Isaiah* liii, *Psalms* xxii and xlii, *Exodus* xii. 46 and *Zechariah* xii. 10.

Just as the conduct of Pilate is incredible to anyone at all familiar with Roman law and practice, so is it even more incredible that on the eve or first day of the celebration of the Passover the chief priests, elders and scribes should have attended the crucifixion of Jesus to mock and jeer. The records here are obviously in conflict with the circumstances of the period, and seek, with the aim of the 'testimonies', to elaborate, embroider, and turn into a kind of miracle play, to be so readily represented as at Oberammergau, the very small amount of reliable information available.

Thus there could be introduced into the Gospel such embellishments as that while Jesus was on the cross the whole land was shrouded in darkness in the middle of the day. Even the sun could not look upon what was happening. At the moment of Jesus's death there was a violent earthquake. The rocks were rent, and the very curtain covering the Holy of Holies in the Temple was ripped from top to bottom. Even the tombs of the saints buried near the city were flung open. The corpses rose up and walked about Jerusalem, seen by many. In *Matthew* the resurrection of Jesus is made practicable by the descent of an angel, who rolls away the stone from the entrance of the tomb and sits on it. This is pure mythology, which continues with the resurrection narratives, and finally – with *Luke* – the visible ascent of Jesus to heaven in broad daylight (*Acts* i. 9-10). I am not for a moment suggesting that the tomb in which Jesus had been laid was not found open and empty when it was visited by women of his company early on the third day, only that a good reason for it did not have to be supernormal.[2]

In the age when these miraculous things were set down they were deemed quite appropriate, indeed essential. Without such adornments it would be felt that the reporter did not know his job, and was failing to do justice to his hero. People did not think so much in terms of facts and literal truth, as we do, but of forces working on one side with the Goodies and on the other with the Baddies. These forces had to be shown to have been in operation miraculously or magically, in the march of events. If they did not manifest themselves how was one to credit the exalted status of the hero?

When we read these Gospel accounts, therefore, what has to be present to our minds is Greek sacred drama, or in modern terms the morality play, fairy tale and pantomime, rather than the cautious sobriety of the careful historian and biographer. The effect on the emotions is imperative. Unless the fictitious factors and spiritual intrusions are given their place, our emotions would not be sufficiently aroused. We have to be moved both to hiss and to applaud. It is a responsibility on us to adapt ourselves to this larger-than-life mode of presentation, but not to be deceived by it. We are not to conclude that the Gospel accounts are wholly fictitious; but we have to seek dispassionately and with the greatest care for the reliable elements.

I have need to clarify these matters at this juncture for two reasons. First I must say that my investigations and critical statements are in no way due to hostile or cynical motives, much less frivolous ones, as the orthodox Christian believer might incline to affirm. My heart, as well as mind, has been involved for upwards of sixty years. Secondly, I have to try to induce the reader to govern his views by the standards of another age, so that he does not judge in the manner either of the modern believer or sceptic. Only thus can he come near to the truth.

A vital essential, therefore, is to familiarise ourselves with such records as are available from the ancient world for purposes of comparison. There are scholars, many of them Christian, who know about such records but for religious reasons ignore them. I am speaking of course of students of the classics, which too many of the clergy are not nowadays.

When we read of the resurrection and ascension of Jesus, as an affirmation of the Gospels, what we should be asking ourselves is, whether this kind of climax to the life of a famous person is unique, or has parallels in the ancient Graeco-Roman literature. We find the answer to be that the ascension to heaven of notable persons was featured in such literature.

Dionysius of Halicarnassus in his *Roman Antiquities* speaks of the passing of the two founders of the Roman race. Of the first he tells us, 'But the body of Aeneas could nowhere be found, and some conjectured that he had been translated to the gods.'[3] Regarding the second (Romulus), he states: 'The more mythical writers say that as he was holding an assembly [Gr. *ekklesia*] in the camp, darkness descended upon him out of a clear sky... he disappeared, and they believe that he was caught up by father Ares.'[4] Plutarch (first century AD) in his *Parallel Lives* develops the theme of the passing of Romulus. He disappeared at a place called the Goats' Marsh, when suddenly the sun was darkened and the day turned into night, while a terrible storm arose. The senators then told the people 'to honour and worship Romulus, as one taken up to the gods, and who, after having been a good prince, was now to be to them a propitious deity.' This was then confirmed by Julius Proculus, a patrician friend of Romulus. He testified on oath that he had encountered Romulus after his passing. The latter was travelling on the road dressed in shining and flaming armour. When Julius chided him for leaving them so abruptly and without explanation, Romulus made answer:

> It pleased the gods, O Proculus, that after we had remained a reasonable time among men, and built a city, the greatest in the world both in empire and glory, we should again return to heaven from whence we came. But be of good heart, and let the Romans know that by the exercise of temperance and fortitude they shall arrive at the highest pitch of human power, and we will be to you the propitious God Quirinius.

So settled was this imagination, especially among the Romans of the first century AD, that the great philosopher Seneca could joke about it in his *Apocolocyntosis*. 'You demand evidence?' he says.

'Right. Ask the man who saw Drusilla *en route* for heaven. He will tell you that he saw Claudius [the emperor] going up too, cloppety-cloppety in his usual fashion [he was lame]. That man just can't help seeing what goes on in the skies.'[5]

Among the Jews there was an inclination of some to convey that a like experience had been granted to the great lawgiver Moses. It was described in a Hebrew work, of which only Greek and Latin reflections survive, which is known as the *Assumption of Moses*. But to safeguard the humanity of Moses so that no one should be tempted to adore him as divine, his exodus was seen in two fashions by Joshua and Caleb: in one he was taken up to heaven while in the other he was lost to view in a mountain ravine. Reference is made to this by Clement of Alexandria at the end of the second century in his *Miscellanies* (*Strom.* vi. 15). But already in the previous century the Jewish historian Josephus was aware of the legend. He tells us:

> And while he [i.e. Moses] bade farewell to Eleazar [the high priest] and Joshua, and was yet communing with them, a cloud of a sudden descended upon him and he disappeared in a ravine. But he has written of himself in the sacred books that he died, for fear lest they should venture to say that by reason of his surpassing virtue he had gone back to the Deity.[6]

We are well advised, therefore, in the case of Jesus to recognise that there has been an appropriate embellishment of the circumstances, especially in *Matthew*, in line with the fashion of the time.

The question is how much do we have to discount, and, with so many contradictions and inventions, intensified by doctrinal and polemical considerations, how we reach at least approximate truth.

To this there is a substantially reliable answer. In the first place we can set aside the mythical and miraculous elements, especially those which are peculiar to one Gospel, and analyse the remainder. We can also discount those which resemble what was related of eminent persons by contemporary non-Christians. We shall be very cautious with embellishments which can be traced to other records, especially to the Old Testament. In respect of speeches we shall give little credence to those which could not be overheard for record.

The historical resources must then be brought into play by the modern investigator, particularly in two respects. With the first, he must seek to ascertain what can be gleaned about the social and political scene in Palestine in the period with which we are concerned, and the character and conduct of the leading personalities involved, both Roman and Jewish. How much is what we read in the Gospels consistent with what other sources report? The second aspect is more difficult: it concerns incidental references to matters which could be genuine but lay outside or on the fringe of the Gospel writer's primary concerns, and which he does not elaborate. A case in point is where *Luke* has Jesus sent by Pontius Pilate for examination by Herod Antipas, which concludes with the unexplained statement, 'That day Herod and Pilate became friends with one another; for previously they had been at enmity.' (*Luke* xxiii. 12)

The impression we have of Pilate in the Gospels is that he was a weak and vacillating individual who was trapped against his will into condemning to death a Jew for claiming the Jewish throne. This is not how other sources closer to the circumstances depict him. Fortunately one of these sources was actually a contemporary of Pontius Pilate when he was governor of Judea and in a position to speak with full knowledge. This was no less a person than Herod Agrippa, later himself king of the Jews as Agrippa I. He was a close friend of the Emperor Gaius and was at Rome when the Jewish philosopher Philo of Alexandria was seeking to restrain Gaius from having his statue set up in the Temple at Jerusalem. In his *Embassy to Gaius*,[7] Philo gives *in extenso* the plea of Agrippa on behalf of the Jews to dissuade the emperor from his design. It is in this work that the references to Pilate occur. He is referred to as 'naturally inflexible, a blend of self-will and relentlessness, a man noted for vindictiveness and furious temper.' Is this the Pilate of the Gospels? Further on it is stated how the Jews knew Pilate as governor: the catalogue lists 'briberies, insults, robberies, outrages and wanton injuries, executions without trial constantly repeated, ceaseless and supremely grievous cruelty.'

The first-century Jewish historian Josephus, a friend of Vespasian and Titus, depicts Pilate similarly in various incidents he describes. Almost at the end of his governorship, before he was dismissed from office, and about the time of the affair of Jesus, there had appeared among the Samaritans one who claimed to be their Messiah (*Taheb*), and who led a crowd to the holy Mount Gerizim where he had said he would reveal the sacred vessels of the Tabernacle which Moses was believed to have buried there. How did Pilate act on this occasion? Did he seek to evade responsibility? Fully in character he sent a strong force to cut down the devotees, and had the leaders put to death.[8] Josephus fully confirms that Pilate was the kind of man Agrippa says he was, and not at all a noble Roman unlucky enough to be out-smarted by tricky merciless Jews. 'In the mouth of two witnesses shall every word be established.'

We have to apprehend what the Gospel writers state, but frequently seek to evade, that a claim to be the Messiah (Christ) of the Jews, descended from David, was a claim to be their king. Since the Romans at this time had incorporated Judea in the Roman province of Syria no one was permitted to make such a claim without the imperial sanction. It must be clearly understood that when Jesus rode into Jerusalem to the plaudits of the multitude as king of the Jews this was on his part a deliberate act of high treason, the crime of *laesa majestas*, blasphemy of the divine Caesar, punishable by death. There are a number of examples in the Roman records. This circumstance being brought to Pilate's attention he was bound to crucify Jesus promptly. And, as justice required, the nature of the crime was affixed to the cross: 'This is Jesus king of the Jews.' Why do the Christian authorities exhibit no awareness of Roman Law at that time? And of course it was no crime at all in Jewish Law to claim to be the Messiah. What a burden of guilt the Church carries!

The whitewashing of Pilate and the aim to pin the blame for the death of Jesus on the Jews reveals itself to any impartial person as a design of antisemitic Graeco-Roman Christians. It not only expressed their animus against the Jews, very strong among the Hellenes at the time as many records bear witness,[9] but also – since the Jews had revolted against the Romans urged on by a political-Messianic motivation – reflected the concern of the Christians outside Palestine to dissociate their own Messianism from any taint of conspiracy against the Empire. The fact had been that until Christianity had become a new religion completely divorced from Judaism, around the close of the first century AD, the majority of Christians had been implacably hostile to the Roman Empire, as reflected in the *Book of Revelation*. The Romans refused to license Christianity as a genuine religion, and treated the sect as sinister and subversive. The action of Nero in accusing the Christians of setting fire to Rome had some warrant in the predictions of the followers of Jesus of its doom by fire. Hence, after the Jewish War with Rome, the apologetic efforts of Christian literature in the Roman Empire.

We come then to the part played by the Jewish authorities in the trial and execution of Jesus, and the endeavour of the Gospel writers to put the blame on the Jews and exonerate Pilate. Pilate both pronounces Jesus innocent, when in Roman law he was decidedly guilty, and also gives the Jewish authorities a choice to doom Jesus or Barabbas, so that responsibility rests with the Jews. Pilate acts in a manner not only contrary to his recorded behaviour, as we have shown, but also in grave violation of his official responsibilities.

I do not propose at this juncture to go into details; but it is evident that the chief priests and their supporters are made to represent the position of the Jewish nation, which is quite untrue. By intention, those who are favourable to Jesus are simply called 'the people' rather than 'the Jewish people'. The priests do not want to arrest Jesus on the feast day because they fear the people. What people are they, if not the Jews? So Jesus is taken and arraigned at night, so that the populace should be in ignorance.

NOTES AND REFERENCES

1. A first cousin of Jesus, Simeon son of Cleopas, is reputed to have survived until the beginning of the second century, while grandsons of Jude, the brother of Jesus, are said to have been interrogated by the Emperor Domitian near the close of the first century.
2. See my book *The Passover Plot*.
3. *Ant. Rom.* i. 64. 4.
4. Ibid. ii. 56. 2.
5. See J. P. V. D. Balsdon, *The Romans*, pp. 257ff.
6. Josephus, *Antiquities*, Bk. IV. 325-326.
7. Philo, *Embassy to Gaius*, xxxvi and xxxviii (Loeb Vol. X).
8. Josephus, *Antiq*. Bk. XVIII. 85-87.
9. For instance, the 'pogroms' in Caesarea and Alexandria.

7.

Turning to the Gentiles

We have seen how there was a certain shaping of the Gospels to the attitudes and prejudices of the Christian communities in the various parts of the Roman Empire in which they originated. These communities were mainly non-Jewish in membership; and we should appreciate that the converts had been gained mainly by listening to missionaries and preachers. The Gospels in their regional forms were thus secondary, taking on the colouring of their religious and social environment in certain respects. This is brought home to us from the remains recovered of several of the uncanonical gospels. But even in the canonical ones, those inaccurately described as synoptic, the evidences are to be found.

I may illustrate this from passages which have no doctrinal or ethnic emphasis. In the Sermon on the Mount the teaching of Jesus concludes with a simile, the building of a house by a wise man and by a foolish one. In the natural conditions represented by *Matthew* the former builds his house on rock, while the latter builds his on sand. But in the conditions represented by *Luke* the wise man digs deep into the ground until he finds rock, but the second man builds his house not on sand but upon soil without foundations. Elsewhere, in the account of the healing of a paralytic by Jesus, *Mark* conveys that the man's friends let him down to Jesus in the rooms below by breaking up the flat roof. But in *Luke* these friends are represented as removing tiles.

Such things, though minor, are worthy of note. What is much more remarkable, however, especially in the Synoptic Gospels, is what a surprisingly large measure of non-Gentile and anti-Paulinist Christian material these Gospels contain. We have already to an extent noted this in Chapter 4, and it is very encouraging historically. It conveys that as regards these Gospels the teaching of Jesus in its personal and native Jewish character had substantially been preserved, even when it was in flat contradiction of what Pauline Christianity was now teaching. It was simply too authoritative to be altered or suppressed, though often it was ignored. Thus the written gospel still preserved the contentions of those who represented the immediate disciples of Jesus, those who have come to be called Judaisers, in claiming that Jesus had required the observance of the Law of Moses down to the last jot and tittle. Paul and his supporters could quote no word of Jesus to the contrary. It is hardly surprising, then, that the teachings of the Christ are almost entirely ignored in the Pauline epistles. Indeed, Paul declared that he did not want to know the human Jesus.

However, in writing to the Roman church which he had not founded and which was substantially composed of Jews at that time, Paul does allow himself to state that Jesus had been a Jew, born of the tribe of Judah and of the house of David. He evidently knew nothing of any virgin birth. Paul claimed that converts from the Gentiles had by faith become naturalised Israelites (*Rom.* xi; *Eph.* ii). He had taken the initiative in evangelising them, as the *Acts of the Apostles* and the Pauline epistles leave us in no manner of doubt. This development was entirely unexpected by those who had been the immediate followers of Jesus who were practising Jews, and by the multitude of Jews who adhered to their teaching (*Acts* xxi. 20). The result was a heated controversy, and a determined effort to induce the converts from the Gentiles to become full proselytes to Judaism. Evangelical Christians, with their chant of 'Free from the Law, O happy condition', have completely misunderstood what animated the 'Judaisers'. They have not been aware of the Jewish conviction at that time, as Jesus was aware of it, that the Messianic Age could not dawn until all Israel observed the Torah in faithfulness. Those who violated God's Law were therefore delaying the Redemption.

Eventually, to avoid a complete split, and repudiation of the Gentile believers, they were allowed to be accepted into fellowship as half-proselytes, Gentiles who were God-fearers, who repudiated idolatry and kept the primeval Laws of Noah (*Acts* xv), but had not formally become Israelites. They were to be received as 'the stranger within the gates'. Paul did not relish this, as we can see from his letter to the Galatian communities, and it would lead to the severance of the Pauline churches from allegiance to the Apostolic Council at Jerusalem, of which Jacob (James) the brother of Jesus was president.

Paul broke with the Jesus of history, whom he referred to as 'the other Jesus', but after his death the situation was somewhat retrieved by the Synoptic Gospels. Their Jesus had not only observed the Torah; he had remained within the boundaries of Israel throughout his ministry. He never entered the house of a Gentile or an alien city. When, exceptionally, Jesus cured the daughter of a Canaanite woman, he did not go to her house, and it was emphasised that the cure was allowable because of the special circumstances (*Matt.* xv. 21-28).

When Jesus had sent out his disciples to proclaim the near advent of the Kingdom of God he gave them strict instructions not to go in the way of the Gentiles, not even into any Samaritan city (*Matt.* x. 5-7). No Gentile believer would have wished to invent such details, and they should therefore be treated as factual. But in the Gentile churches they were felt to be so uncomfortable that they do not appear in *Mark* and *Luke*. And even in *Matthew* it was felt necessary to provide a modifying postscript, which read: 'Go, therefore, and make disciples of all the Gentiles, immersing them in the name of the Father, and the Son, and the Holy Spirit, teaching them to observe whatever I have commanded you. I shall indeed be constantly at your side until the Consummation of the Age.' The terms of this postscript make it very clear that this was no utterance of Jesus.

The comparable passage in *Mark* is also a later addition, as has long been known to scholars. The Gospel actually breaks off abruptly at *Mark* xvi. 8, where the women of Jesus's company flee in fear when they find his sepulchre empty. Yet this substitute ending in *Mark* has furnished the mandate for the Christian missionary enterprises of subsequent times in language that Jesus never used, which I quote here in the Authorised Version: 'Go ye into all the world, and preach the Gospel to every creature. He that believeth and is baptized shall be saved; but he that believeth not shall be damned.' (*Mark* xvi. 15-16) We may never know how this Gospel really ended.

It is obvious that had these concluding utterances of Jesus been known to those who had companied with him there would have been no conflict over the reception of Gentiles into the primitive Church representing faithful Israel. They would have settled the matter out of hand. And quite apart from the Apostle Paul, how welcome such sayings of Jesus would have been to his principal disciple Peter, who must be supposed to have heard them personally. When he was challenged by his fellow-apostles and brethren for having visited and accepted the conversion of the Roman centurion Cornelius and his household, though he was a God-fearer and not an idolater, he could have settled the matter immediately by quoting Jesus. Instead we have an elaborate story of visions given to Peter and to Cornelius to justify what took place (*Acts* x).

Jesus had insisted that his mission was to the lost sheep of the house of Israel, and in the capacity of Messiah (Christ) this was a vital part of his function. These lost sheep had to be restored to the Jewish community as the People of God, so that Israel could fulfil its Messianic function to the nations. This is why we have the stories Jesus told (*Luke* xv) of the Lost Sheep, the Lost Coin and the Prodigal Son. Such stories could be employed later in the churches as missionary aids for the salvation of individual sinners everywhere; but this was not why Jesus had related them. Personal salvation was a doctrine of the Gentiles very widespread in the Roman Empire. Individuals were prepared to undergo a variety of ordeals and initiatory rites to assure their salvation, and at great expense. Such salvation was quite out of reach of the slaves and the poor. This was why salvation through the blood of Christ was so appealing to this class of Gentile. The Paulinists were able to offer it to them without money and without price. It has been the sacrificial aspect of the crucifixion that has endeared Jesus to sinners down the centuries: 'He did it for me.'

But in seeking out exclusively the Jewish sinner there was a greater purpose that Jesus was serving. He would lose no opportunity to reclaim such an individual to the discomfort of the Scribes and Pharisees. Some of them could complain, 'This man receiveth sinners, and eateth with them.' One such sinner was a man named Zacchaeus, who had stooped to enrich himself by acting against his people as a tax-gatherer for the heathen Roman government in Judea, chief of the hated *publicani*.

The story goes, that on the way to Jerusalem at the close of his life Jesus had invited himself to stay with this man, who was so overjoyed that he repented and offered restitution and the donation of half his fortune to charity. The Jewish populace to whom Zacchaeus was anathema were concerned that Jesus should lodge with such a vile person. But he had responded: 'Salvation has come to this house today, since here too is *a son of Abraham*.' The italics are mine.

That such words were characteristic of Jesus is further confirmed by the lost *Gospel of the Hebrews*, a very early Aramaic Gospel of which only a few passages have been preserved in quotation. One incident from it was inserted in the Latin version of Origen's *Commentary on Matthew*, xix. It also concerns a rich Jew in the company of another who had approached Jesus. As regards the second, he had wanted to know how he could be sure of participating in the life of the Messianic Age (the Kingdom of God on earth). Jesus had told him to keep the Commandments (i.e. the Decalogue). The young man insisted that he had kept them. But was that all? Jesus then told him to distribute his riches to the poor.[1] In the way the story was told in the Hebrew Gospel, Jesus had finally said to the man, 'How sayest thou, I have performed the Law and the Prophets, seeing that it is written *in the Law*, Thou shalt love thy neighbour as thyself. And, behold many of thy brethren, *sons of Abraham*, are clad with dung, dying of hunger, and thy house is full of much goods, and there goeth out therefrom nought at all unto them.'

It is of the greatest importance to the understanding of Jesus that there should have been preserved, even in the Gentile Christian communities, sayings and teachings of Jesus which reveal him as a practising Jew functioning exclusively within and in relation to the Jewish people, and in no sense the founder of a new religion.

Jesus might therefore be accused of being insular and narrowly Judaistic, an apparent weakness which the Greek Gospels sought to an extent to play down by certain omissions and additions. What the non-Jewish Christians, especially the Greeks with their strong individualism, had the utmost difficulty in grasping, was that Judaism with its Messianic message represented a collective ideology, the mission not of a person to persons for the saving of individual souls, but of a nation to the nations. Thus the emphasis of Jesus on his disciples going only to Jews cast no slur on Gentiles nor suggested any superiority of the Chosen People. It was a policy which embraced the love of God for all mankind, as set forth by the Hebrew prophets. Until all Israel was redeemed the nations of the world could not be saved, for the nation of Israel had been called and chosen to be the instruments of the salvation of the nations. God had told Abraham that in his descendants all the nations of the earth would be blessed.[2]

Jesus knew and believed this. His function was to bring back to the fold Jews who had gone astray, because only so could salvation come to the Gentiles (all the nations of the world), by the instrumentality of redeemed Israel. Jesus was Judaistic *because* he cared for the Gentiles.

The Church got things all wrong, since this was not grasped or understood, even though the information is plainly there within the covers of the Bible.

NOTES AND REFERENCES

1. See *Matt.* xix.16-24, *Mark* x.17-25, *Luke* xviii.18-25.
2. *Gen.* xii. 3, xxii. 18, xxvi. 4.

8.

Back to First Base

There is something deeply moving in the Christian conception of the Messiah as reflected in Handel's beautiful oratorio. It is a kind of Prometheus story, but much more charged with an emotional humanity. The central figure arouses in us the strongest feeling of sorrow, pity and love, and his experiences of rejection and triumph stir in us anger and rejoicing. And we are the more involved and concerned because what takes place is for us and because of us.

There is, of course, an element of truth in this drama. If it were not so it would not affect us so strongly. But the Christian emphasis has concentrated on the Man (singular), while the Jewish emphasis is on the Man (collective). The Messiah for mankind is the People of Israel, not alas represented by the State of Israel. The soul of Israel has indeed awaited a personal Messiah, her king, as the signal that her own nightmare of suffering was coming to an end, and would be vindicated by the Peace and Justice which now would reign throughout the world.

When the harp of Judah sounded, [wrote Rabbi Mendes] thrilled with the touch of inspiration Divine, among the echoes it waked in the human heart were those sweet sounds whose witcheries transport the soul into the realms of happiness. That melody has been our source of courage, our solace and our strength, and in all our wanderings we have sung it. It is the music of the Messianic age, the triumph-hymn to be one day thundered by all humanity, the real psalm of life as mankind shall sing it when Israel's world-task of teaching it shall have been accomplished. Its harmony is the harmony of the families of the earth, at last in peace, at last united in brotherhood, at last happy in their return to the One Great Father.[1]

56

But let us look back to the Jewish Bible, the Bible which was the inspiration of Jesus. In *Genesis* the call of Abraham the Hebrew was for the ultimate purpose of the well-being of all mankind through his descendants, as we have seen. The Prophets took up this theme at a time when Israel was surrounded by hostile powers, and their vision of the future seemed most unlikely to be realised.

And it shall come to pass in the last days, that the mountain of the Lord's house shall be... exalted above the hills; and all nations shall flow unto it. And many people shall go and say, Come ye, and let us go up to the mountain of the Lord, to the house of the God of Jacob; and he will teach us of his ways, and we will walk in his paths. For out of Zion shall go forth the Law, and the word of the Lord from Jerusalem. And he shall judge among the nations, and shall rebuke many peoples: and they shall beat their swords into ploughshares, and their spears into scythes: nation shall not lift up sword against nation, neither shall they learn war any more. (*Isa.*ii.2-4; *Micah* iv.1-4)

There shall come people, and the inhabitants of many cities; and the inhabitants of one city shall go to another, saying, Let us go speedily to pray before the Lord, and to seek the Lord of hosts: I will go also. Yea, many peoples and strong nations shall come to seek the Lord of hosts in Jerusalem, and to pray before the Lord... In those days it shall come to pass, that ten men shall take hold out of all languages of the nations, even shall take hold of the skirt of him that is a Jew, saying, We will go with you: for we have heard that God is with you. (*Zech.* viii. 20-23)

Remember ye not the former things, neither consider the things of old. Behold, I will do a new thing; now it shall spring forth... I will even make a way in the wilderness, and rivers in the desert... to give drink to my people, my chosen. This people have I formed for myself; they shall shew forth my praise. (*Isa.* xliii. 18-21)

(The last quotation is from the group of the so-called Servant Psalms, where Israel is likened to God's Servant and the instrument of His redemption.)

Such ideas had come strongly back into currency among the Jews as a result of the persecution they had suffered in the second century BC at the hands of the Seleucid king, Antiochus IV. The effect was sharply to reverse the tendency that had been in evidence since the time of Alexander the Great, to forsake Jewish exclusiveness and embrace Greek culture, even to the extent of religious syncretism and the adoption of pagan practices. But Antiochus had gone too far in his attempt to abolish Judaism, stimulating a resistance movement among pious Jews, which had been a natural reaction to such apostasy. In the end what had triumphed had been a Jewish revivalism, carrying with it a reassessment of the Jewish world mission in the light of the Biblical records and prophetic intimations.

During the next century Judaism became strongly propagandist, not so much as a *religion* – Judaism did not go in for theology – but rather as a spiritual and political philosophy and way of life. It had books not statues.

Various non-Jewish writers of the period make reference to it, as I have described in other books.[2] Basic was the proclamation of the one and sole God, without form or substance, who would reward the righteous and punish sinners, but was always a God of love, a true Father. There went with this affirmation a developing Messianism which stressed the salutary function of Israel as God's son and servant under a ruler of His choice, and warned of impending wrath and judgement on the evildoers before the advent of the Golden Age.

In a manner which was characteristic of antique propaganda, revered alien literature was taken over, altered and interpolated, to get the message across. Additions were made to the texts of the famed *Sibylline Oracles*. They were made to speak of the Jews as 'a holy race of god-fearing men', 'a royal tribe', and 'the people of the great God... they who are to be the guides of life to all mankind'.[3] Such material was to be multiplied until well into the second century AD by both Jews and Christians, and there was also denunciation directed especially against the proud and pagan Roman Empire. We may give here two typical passages:

> But when Rome shall rule over Egypt, though still delaying, then shall the great kingdom of the immortal King appear among men, and a holy king shall come who shall have rule over the whole earth for all ages of the course of time. Then shall implacable wrath fall upon the men of Latium... Ah, wretched me, when shall that day come, and the judgement of immortal God, the great king? Yet still be ye builded ye cities, and all adorned with temples and theatres, with market squares and images of gold, silver and stone, that so ye may come to the

day of bitterness. For it shall come when the smell of brimstone shall pass upon all men.

Near at hand
Is the end of the world, and the last day,
And judgement of immortal God for such
As are both called and chosen. First of all
Inexorable wrath shall fall on Rome:
A time of blood and wretched life shall come.
Woe, woe to thee, O land of Italy,
Great barbarous nation... [4]

This kind of apocalypticism, of which there is a typical example in the New Testament, prevailed roughly between 150 BC and AD 150. It was something which had tremendous repercussions. Never before had there been this concentrated anticipation of the end of the existing world order with all its evils, and its replacement by the just and peaceful Kingdom of God. 'In the days of those kings shall the God of heaven set up a kingdom, which shall never be destroyed.' (*Dan.* ii. 44)

In the first chapter of this book I have mentioned the impression made on me as a Jewish youth by the apocalypticism aroused in many by the circumstances of the First World War. In the Nuclear Age on which we are now embarked prophetic imagination has been no less rife. But in the time with which we are concerned it was a novelty, and with people on the whole being much more superstitious and impressionable in those days the effect was even more telling. A spate of prophetic and admonitory books emanated from the Jewish sectarian seers, often in the names of Israel's Old Testament heroes and credited with being divinely inspired. And certainly in the experiences of Israel – as well as in the world at large – there was no lack of 'signs'.

The reign of the tyrannical gloomy half-pagan tyrant Herod the Great was seen as a portent. There were wars and famines and earthquakes, the martyrdom of many saints. There was the defilement of the Temple of God by avaricious chief priests, the clank of legions as the heathen Romans under their idolatrous rulers took over the world. No wonder that the antiquely-dressed figure of John the Baptist should appear and thunder out warnings, and that the word would go forth to repentant thousands: 'The appointed time has come, and the Kingdom of Heaven is at hand.' It had been many generations since a prophet had appeared in Israel. Before we seek to interpret Jesus these are the circumstances we have to absorb.

Let us cite here only one of the Jewish 'revelations' relating to the reign of Herod.

> And an insolent king will succeed them [i.e. the Hasmoneans], who will not be of the race of the priests, a man bold and shameless [Herod], and he will judge them [the Jews] as they shall deserve. And he shall cut off their chief men with the sword, and he will destroy them in secret places, so that no one may know where their bodies are. He will slay the old and the young, and he will not spare. Then the fear of him will be bitter unto them in their land. And he will execute judgement on them as the Egyptians executed upon them, during thirty and four years, and he will punish them.[5]

Josephus spells out all the details of Herod's conduct in his *Antiquities* (Book XVIII) so that it was no wonder that this monarch was likened to the Pharaoh of the Exodus, and that early Christian legend credited him with the destruction of Jewish infants, building on legends of the birth of Moses.[6]

In the very last year of the king's life zealous young Jews were inspired by religious teachers to hack down the golden eagle which Herod, contrary to Jewish Law, had erected over the gate of the Temple. Many of them were burnt alive on the king's orders, and that same night, reports Josephus, there was an eclipse of the moon. From coins found at Qumran it would appear that about this time a substantial number of the Community of the New Covenant, whom we know as Essenes, returned from their self-imposed exile to their base near the Dead Sea. There they would continue gathering recruits and publishing prophetic and edifying literature until they were forced out by the Roman legions.

We cannot begin to understand the story of Jesus, or Jesus himself, until we have grasped the tremendous impact upon him of the circumstances of his time. It was a Messianic Age, believing itself to be participating in the last great conflict between Good and Evil, Light and Darkness, before the ultimate triumph on earth of the Divine Order. Anything could happen, marvels, miracles, heavenly phenomena, judgements and disasters. And either in imagination or in actuality they were seen or were believed to be happening.

NOTES AND REFERENCES

1. Quoted in *A Book of Jewish Thoughts*.
2. See Hugh J. Schonfield, *Judaism and World Order* and *Those Incredible Christians*.
3. H. N. Bate, *The Sibylline Oracles* (1918).
4. *Sibylline Oracles*, Bks. VIII and III. The sentiments are very representative of primitive Christianity.
5. *Assumption of Moses*, VI. 2-6. Translated by R. H. Charles.
6. See below, Chapter 10.

9.

The Awaited Messiah

Even with the Bible in their hands it is extremely difficult for non-Jews to identify themselves with the imaginations and expectations of the Jewish people at the dawn of the Christian era. Things unprecedented were about to happen, awe-inspiring and miraculous: both an ultimate assault of the forces of Evil inflicting great suffering on Israel, especially on the righteous, and the final triumph of Good with the appearance of the Deliverer, the holy king of the house of David. Yet what was anticipated is very clearly expressed in the prophecy put into the mouth of the priest Zechariah, father of John the Baptist, in *Luke*'s Gospel.

> Blessed be the Lord God of Israel; for he hath visited and redeemed his people, and hath raised up an horn of salvation for us in the house of his servant David; as he spake by the mouth of his holy prophets, which have been since the world began: that we should be saved from our enemies, and from the hand of all that hate us; to perform the mercy promised to our fathers, and to remember his holy covenant; the oath which he sware to our father Abraham, that he would grant unto us, that we being delivered out of the hand of our enemies might serve him without fear, in holiness and righteousness before him, all the days of our life. (*Luke* i. 68-75)

These sentiments are very different from those reflected in many of the Christmas carols, even when they hail the birth of the king of Israel. For Christians, who only think of Jesus as the divine Son of God and saviour of men everywhere, there would seem to be no point in Jesus being born a Jew, or in Palestine, or at the time he manifested himself. He should surely have appeared among Gentiles who believed that gods could appear on earth in human form.

But I am moving too quickly for a correct understanding. First we have to ask why Israel is being hated and persecuted. The prophetic answer is, as we have seen in the last chapter, that redeemed Israel is to be the instrument of the redemption of all nations, of all mankind. Consequently, at the climax of history, the forces of Evil are directed to putting the People of God out of commission by the dual process of spiritual corruption and physical destruction. To counter this, God will send two agents.

The first of these agents will be a new Elijah as a priestly prophet to reconcile parents and children, thus redeeming the basic unity of the family and purifying the ministers of religion from vice and corruption (*Malachi* iii-iv). This first agent, according to the Jewish seers, will be the herald of the second; but his own work will be interrupted because very naturally the forces of Evil will be out to destroy him so that he cannot complete his task. Thus he will die a martyr.

The second agent will be a righteous king of Israel of the house of David. He will be the leader and commander of the nation: he will rally the remnant of his people, the Saints of the Most High, and rout the forces of Evil, but not by evil means, weapons of war. He will 'smite the earth with *the rod of his mouth*, and with *the breath of his lips* shall he slay the wicked' (*Isa.* xi, 4). It will be by the irresistible force of the truths he utters that he will rout the enemy. After this he will inaugurate the Kingdom of God on earth, and according to the prophetic fancy all the righteous dead of Israel will reap the reward of their loyalty to God and of their self-sacrifice by being restored to life to reign with the Messiah over redeemed mankind. A typical description is the following:

> And it shall come to pass after these things, when the time of the advent of the Messiah is fulfilled and he will return in glory, then all who have fallen asleep in hope of him shall rise again. And it will come to pass at that time that the treasuries will be opened in which is preserved the number of the souls of the righteous, and they will come forth, and a multitude of souls will be seen together in one assemblage of one thought, and the first will rejoice and the last will not be grieved. For he knows that the time has come of which it is said that it is the consummation of the times.[1]

We have given here only a brief summary of the concepts that pious circles in Israel, Essenes, Pharisees, etc., were putting into circulation in numerous books – many of which have been recovered – around the beginning of the Christian era. But as one very clear and positive presentation of the awaited Messiah, which may assist those who only know their Bible, we may quote that which is given in the non-canonical *Psalms of Solomon*. It is a very revealing composition, which every Christian should ponder. After rehearsing the evils that had fallen upon Israel because of the pressure of the evildoers the text continues:

> Behold, O Lord, and raise up unto them their king, the son of David, in the time which thou, O God, knowest, that he may reign over Israel thy servant; and gird him with strength that he may break in pieces them that rule unjustly, and purge Jerusalem, with wisdom and with righteousness, from the heathen that trample her down to destroy her.
>
> He shall thrust out sinners from the inheritance, utterly destroy the proud spirit of the sinners, and as potters' vessels with a rod of iron shall be break in pieces all their substance. He shall destroy the ungodly nations with the word of his mouth, so that at his rebuke the nations may flee before him, and he shall convict the sinners in the thoughts of their heart.
>
> And he shall gather together a holy people, whom he shall lead in righteousness; and shall judge the tribes of the people that hath been sanctified by the Lord his God. And he shall not suffer iniquity to lodge in their midst; and none that knoweth wickedness shall dwell with them. For he shall take knowledge of them, that they be all the sons of their God, and shall divide them upon the earth according to their tribes.
>
> And the sojourner and the stranger shall dwell with them no more. He shall judge the nations and the peoples with the wisdom of his righteousness. Selah.
>
> And he shall possess the nations of the heathen to serve him beneath his yoke; and he shall glorify the Lord in a place to be seen of the whole earth; and he shall judge Jerusalem and make it holy, even as it was in the days of old. So that the nations may come from the ends of the earth to see his glory, bringing as gifts her sons that had fainted, and may see the glory of the Lord, wherewith God hath glorified her.
>
> And a righteous king and taught of God is he that reigneth over them; and there shall be no iniquity in his days in their midst, for all shall be holy and their king is the Lord Messiah.

For he shall not put his trust in horse and rider and bow, nor shall he multiply unto himself gold and silver for war, nor by ships shall he gather confidence for the day of battle. The Lord himself is his King, and the hope of him that is strong in the hope of God.

And he shall have mercy upon all the nations that come before him in fear. For he shall smite the earth with the word of his mouth even for evermore. He shall bless the people of the Lord with wisdom and gladness.

He himself also is pure from sin, so that he may rule a mighty people, and rebuke princes and overthrow sinners by his word. And he shall not faint all his days, because he leaneth upon his God; for God shall cause him to be mighty through the spirit of holiness, and wise through the counsel of understanding, with might and righteousness.

And the blessing of the Lord is with him in might, and his hope in the Lord shall not faint. And who can stand up against him, who is mighty in his works and strong in the fear of God, tending the flock of the Lord with faith and righteousness? And he shall suffer none among them to faint in their pasture. In holiness shall he lead them all, and there shall be no pride among them that any should be oppressed. This is the majesty of the king of Israel, which God hath appointed to raise him up over the house of Israel, to instruct him.

His words shall be purified above fine gold, yea, above the choicest gold. In the congregation will he judge among the peoples, the tribes of them that have been sanctified. His words shall be as the words of the holy ones in the midst of the peoples that have been sanctified.

Blessed are they that shall be born in those days, to behold the blessing of Israel which God shall bring to pass in the gathering together of the tribes. May God hasten his mercy towards Israel! May he deliver us from the abomination of unhallowed adversaries! The Lord, he is our King from henceforth and even for evermore.[2]

Much else of a similar character might be quoted from Jewish extra-canonical sources of the period. As a consequence of such preaching and teaching, multitudes were convinced that the Climax of the Ages had arrived. Signs were being noted and rumours were rife. The expectations were somewhat varied, according to sectarian preferences, but they also had a great deal in common. One body could anticipate two successive Messiahs, the first priestly and the second regal, while another looked for a royal Messiah with a priestly forerunner. There was also a belief in the arrival of a prophet like Moses, and among the mystics the anticipation that the primordial Son of Man in whose likeness Adam was formed would incarnate again. The redemptive personalities tended to become fused. But there was not among them any belief that God would walk the earth in human form. If there had been no influx into the Church of pagan Gentiles to whom such concepts were familiar there would have been no doctrine of the deity of Jesus.

The conviction that was the most prominent was that which identified the Messiah as a holy king of the house of David. There were a good many at the dawn of the Christian era who could claim descent from King David, and some among them could hardly fail to have questioned which of their branches would bear the Sprout who would prove to be he that should come.

We learn in the Gospels of one pious member of the family, named Joseph, who would appear to have nourished the expectation that it could be his first-born son whom he called Jesus (Joshua). There could be some substance in the tradition that his wife Mary (Miriam) had had a vision to this effect. But we have to be very careful in according historicity to the birth stories of both Jesus and John the Baptist, because – and we have seen – they bear such a strong likeness to contemporary legends relating to the births of Abraham and Moses, with some reflections of the nativity stories of the biblical heroes Samson and Samuel.

Anyone at this time, responding in earnest to the prevailing excitement and speculation, who might claim to be the Messiah, would have needed diligently to apply himself to learning both about the Messiah's character and function. He would have had little to go upon except the current imaginations and interpretations of his rôle, since no one previously had presented himself as Messiah. So far as it is practicable to ascertain, Jesus was the first to do so. There is no evidence that the heroic Judas of Galilee at the beginning of the Christian era had asserted that he was the Messiah, though one of his sons – Menahem – did so at the time of the Jewish revolt against the Romans in AD 66. Neither, it may be considered, did John the Baptist claim to be the priestly Messiah, though this was held by multitudes of his followers.

We do not know when the seed was sown in the mind of Jesus that he himself might be the Messiah. It could well have been when he was a small boy, as a result of what was told him by the father whom he adored, or in response to the excited Last Days atmosphere in evidence all around him. From what is recorded of him as a man he was very devout, and highly sensitive and impressionable.

A story is told in *Luke*, which may have some basis in fact, of a visit to Jerusalem at the Passover on which Jesus at twelve years of age had accompanied his parents. When the time came to return home the boy was found to be missing after the party had completed the first day's travel. His distraught father and mother went back to the city, and at last after three days he was discovered in the Temple with the Jewish sages. When his parents had chided him Jesus had expressed his surprise and naively replied, 'Why were you looking for me? Didn't you know that I must be about my Father's business?'

The impression we are given is that Jesus had seized a golden opportunity to obtain information he needed at the most competent Jewish level. He was 'both listening to the sages, and asking them questions'. This is not, of course, how later Christians interpreted the incident. They depict him as a show-off, overwhelming the doctors of the Law with his superior spiritual knowledge. The writers of the apocryphal gospels go even further. They depict the boy Jesus as an *enfant terrible*, a most unpleasant religious prig, putting his teachers at school to shame by demonstrating their ignorance.

It is surely preferable, and much more probable, to believe that this young scion of the house of David was genuinely and anxiously seeking to learn all he could about the Messiah because in his childhood imagination the promised Deliverer might be himself.

Of course Jesus had known nothing of the myths and legends attaching to his birth, such as we find in *Matthew* and *Luke*. These, as we have seen, largely imitate those which were current relating to the births of Israel's heroes with some borrowing from current non-Jewish myths. Such embellishments of the Jesus story, significant as they are, had not existed in his lifetime.

But as we study the Gospels in relation to the teaching of Jesus it is very clear – at least it has been to myself – that not only had he been able to formulate a very positive concept of the Messiah's function, but also a well thought out plan of action to carry it into effect. This was a great, and indeed a singular achievement, demanding very high qualities of imagination and resolution, and also a considerable period of determined inquiry.

History tells us later of other claimants of the Messiahship, especially the militant Bar-Cochba and, nearer to our time, the mystic Shaboathai Zevi. None of them exhibits the self-negating and warm-hearted apprehension of the office that we discover with Jesus, and which the Church subsequently failed to comprehend. He deeply loved his nation, and understood that Israel was the ultimate Messiah for all nations. It was his function, therefore, at personal cost and suffering to reclaim his people for their mission. Towards the end he nearly despaired of success.

The records are silent about what Jesus was doing in his youth and early manhood, and there have been many guesses about his activities. What we can be very safe in saying is that these years were largely devoted to intensive research and self-preparation. There were apocalyptic books in circulation as well as the books of the Bible, and we can now see from recovered Essene writings much with which Jesus appears to have been familiar. When his call came, and he took the stage, his function and course of action were already reasonably clear. This is evident from the plans he put into operation, which show signs of prior consideration.

NOTES AND REFERENCES

1. *Apocalypse of Baruch*, xxx. 1-3 (translated by R. H. Charles).
2. *Psalms of Solomon*, xvii. 23-51 (edited and translated by H. E. Ryle and M. R. James). The *Revelation* in the New Testament exhibits this kind of Messianic consciousness in relation to Jesus.

10.

When and Whence?

The moment in history which finally confirmed to Jesus that the exalted office of Messiah had been conferred upon him came when he joined the throng to be dipped in the Jordan by the strident Elijah-like prophet John the son of Zechariah. All the Gospels are agreed on this, and in some texts the words that came to Jesus when he rose out of the water were those of *Psalm* ii, which declared him king, and thus God's chosen son: 'I have anointed my king on Zion the hill of my holiness... Thou art my son; this day have I begotten thee.' But of course what Jesus felt or heard at this solemn moment was locked in his own breast. Imagination is seeking to communicate the Messianic significance of that moment.

For this very reason it is essential at this point to come down out of the clouds and take a pedestrian view of what piety describes as the Advent. Both the Trinitarian formula and Messianic mythology have made this very difficult. There is a solemnity and a glory which have invested the circumstances of Jesus's origin; and it is with great reluctance and through stark necessity that we must break the spell. But the result will alert us to matters of consequence which otherwise we may miss, and enable us to free ourselves both from ignorance and self-deception. The human limitations of Jesus must command our greater respect because they make his dedication more significant. For a village artisan in humble circumstances it must have called not only for great faith but for great courage to submit himself to so tremendous a responsibility.

The public life of Jesus which committed him to an inner loneliness, as the Gospels make clear, would largely divorce him from his family and friends. They thought of him as smitten by some mental aberration or, less charitably, by demon-possession. At this time his father, it would seem, was no longer living. The relationship between Jesus and his mother is represented as correct and respectful, but hardly as warm and affectionate. His whole being is concentrated on his mission, and his love flows out to the kind of individual, male and female, in whose heart his message can find a lodging.

What has happened to the intercourse between heaven and earth said to have attended his arrival in the world? His mother gives no evidence of awareness of it. His own brothers are ignorant of it; and the villagers of Nazareth seem never to have heard of it. No word of Jesus conveys that anyone had ever told him of angelic choruses and a visit of Magi to his cradle. As evidence of his Messiahship no disciple urges on his behalf that he was other than a native of Galilee.[1]

Here we would seem to come to one of the reasons for the composition of the Nativity legends, the need to meet Jewish objections to the Messiahship of Jesus on grounds that he had not been born in Bethlehem. The belief that the Messiah must come from David's city was widely held in the first century AD, and was based on the prophecy of *Micah* v. 2: 'But thou, Bethlehem Ephrathah... out of thee shall he come forth unto me that is to be the ruler in Israel.'[2] Consequently it had to be claimed that Jesus had in fact been born in Bethlehem. This was conveyed in different ways in *Matthew* and *Luke*.

Matthew allows it to be supposed that the parents of Jesus lived in Bethlehem. It was their home town. After the birth there of the destined Messiah they had first fled with the child to Egypt, and subsequently had settled at Nazareth in Galilee, because the child's life was still deemed to be in danger from the Herodian ruler of Judea. In this way it had come about that Jesus was domiciled in Galilee, though it was not his native land.

Luke takes a different line altogether. He presents himself as a biographer who is reliable and well-informed. Accordingly he makes great play with his allusions to historical personalities and events. In fact a great deal of his material is window-dressing, culled from various sources, which gives a deceptive impression of authenticity. This applies to the whole Gospel, and not simply to the Nativity stories.

To the challenge about Bethlehem *Luke*'s response is to appear to be more realistic. He acknowledges that the parents of Jesus were resident at Nazareth in Galilee. But special circumstances brought them to Bethlehem just before Mary was due to be delivered. This was the tax levy instituted by the Roman emperor Augustus which called for the registration of every individual in the Empire; for which purpose all individuals away from their ancestral homes were required to return there. Joseph, accordingly, being of the family of David, had to travel to David's birthplace at Bethlehem. The enrolment was a fact of history. Every Jew knew about it, and detested it as being against the Laws of Israel and a virtual reduction to servitude. Josephus records that when it was first instituted the Jews were ready to rise up in arms against the Roman government, and many under the leadership of Judas of Galilee actually did so.[3]

We are thus given two distinct versions in confirmation of the Messiahship of Jesus of how he came to be born in Bethlehem. But the recorded circumstances then give rise to another contradiction, that which relates to the year in which Jesus was born.

In *Matthew* the Messiah's nativity was in the reign of Herod the Great, who died in 4 BC. And from the circumstance that the king, in order to eliminate the infant who was a threat to his throne, ordered the massacre of all the boys in Bethlehem up to the age of two years,[4] it has been argued that this could mean that Jesus must have been born in 7 or 8 BC. But such a deduction assumes two things, first the year in Herod's life in which the visit of the Magi is supposed to have taken place, and second that the incident occurred at all and is not an invention. Regarding the first, we have the information in *Matthew* that while the Holy Family was in Egypt Herod had died. The probability would then be that the asserted massacre of the infants took place around the end of 5 BC. Regarding the second, the whole story could be fictitious, since it would appear to be related to Jewish legends of the birth of Abraham and Moses, as we have partially illustrated.[5] Moreover, there was the Roman report that in AD 66 Tiridates of Parthia went with a train of three Magi laden with presents for Nero, 'whom they worshipped as Lord and God, even as Mithras.'[6]

While *Matthew* positively dates the birth of Jesus near the close of the reign of Herod the Great, *Luke* in his version of that Nativity makes no reference either to the massacre of the infants in Bethlehem or to King Herod's involvement. Instead, his guide to the date of the birth of Jesus is the registration for taxation 'first made when Quirinius was governor of Syria', which brought Joseph and Mary to Bethlehem where Jesus is born. The date is AD 6. Thus there is a clear discrepancy between *Matthew* and *Luke* of twelve or thirteen years, which makes a very big difference to the age of Jesus when he embarked on his mission. Was he about thirty years of age, or in his early forties?[7]

We have to allow that exact chronology arrived at by specialised study is asking rather too much of the Evangelists. The story in line with its objectives was paramount, and external events were introduced as supporting evidence which gave this verisimilitude. It is natural for us now, examining the indications, to wish to reach clearcut conclusions, as others going back to the Church Fathers had sought to do. But what is not commendable is that erudite scholars should bend and twist evidences in support of the view that the New Testament records, assumed to be divinely inspired in a literal sense, must be totally accurate and harmonious.

The Nativity stories are a case in point. Here it was deemed imperative to bring *Luke* into harmony with *Matthew*. This could only be done by endeavouring to establish that the Roman census under Quirinius, cited by *Luke*, had been taken in the lifetime of Herod the Great.

It was known that the census, introduced by the Emperor Augustus, was taken at fourteen-year intervals. What was demanded, therefore, was that the one referred to in *Luke* had been conducted around 9 BC. A notable attempt to demonstrate this was made by Sir William Ramsay, and we may quote a brief summary of his argument.

> He [Ramsay] has established the fact that P. Sulpicius Quirinius was not only *legatus* of Syria in AD 6, when the census – including a valuation – consequent on the organization of Judea as a province of the Empire was taken, but also in the lifetime of Herod (*Luke* i. 5, ii.1), when he was in charge of the operations against the Homanadenses, a tribe in the Cicilian Taurus country, a date which we may fix as 11-7 BC.[8]

But whether Quirinius was available and was in a position to conduct a census during the period when Herod was king of the Jews is not the only hurdle to surmount. What has to be proved is that such a census *was* conducted in Judea during Herod's reign. The evidence is wholly against such a theory. First of all it is clear that the census for taxation to which *Luke* ii. 2 refers as having been made first when Quirinius was governor of Syria was the one in AD 6, for the same author (i.e. *Luke*) speaks of 'the days of the taxing' being the time of the insurrection by Judas of Galilee (*Acts* v. 37). And this we know from Josephus was in AD 6, after the Romans had deposed Herod's son Archelaus, and had taken over the government of Judea. During Herod's reign the Romans did not exercise sovereignty in Judea. Not only, therefore, did they have no right to levy taxes in the country, but also their government was in friendly relations with the Jewish monarchy, and this would be an act of domination. The friendship lasted until Herod's death, a friendship with Augustus that had been long-standing, so that he had made the emperor executor of his will. The relations between Herod and his own Jewish subjects were, on the other hand, so bitter and strained, that possibly nothing less than civil war would have resulted if he had allowed such an alien census for taxation to take place. The outcry was severe enough when the tax was levied in AD 6, and it would have been even worse, and dramatically recorded in Jewish history, if it had happened around 8 or 9 BC.

Relating to the Roman census in AD 6, we must leave the last word with the first-century Jewish historian Josephus. Some significant words are italicised.

Quirinius, a Roman senator... and a man who was extremely distinguished in other respects, arrived in Syria, *dispatched by Caesar to be governor of the nation* [i.e. of the Jews] *and to make an assessment of their property.* Coponius, a man of equestrian rank, was sent along with him *to rule over the Jews with full authority.* Quirinius also visited Judea, *which had been annexed to Syria, in order to make an assessment of the property of the Jews and to liquidate the estate of Archelaus. Although the Jews were at first shocked to hear of the registration of property,*[9] they gradually condescended... to go no further in opposition. But a certain Judas, a Gaulonite... who had enlisted the aid of Zaddok, a Pharisee, threw himself into the cause of rebellion. They said that *the assessment carried with it a status amounting to downright slavery,* no less, and appealed to the nation to make a bid for independence.[10]

Reverting to *Matthew,* it is surely time that Christians should be informed that in Jewish legend when Abraham was born a star was seen in the heavens by the soothsayers of King Nimrod which swallowed up four other stars. This was interpreted as a threat to his dominion. An offer was made to Abraham's father to buy the child in order to kill him. But Terah preserved his son by hiding him in a cave.[11]

A similar story was told, as Josephus relates, of the birth of Moses. Here one of the sacred scribes of the Egyptians announced to Pharaoh that 'there would be born to the Israelites at that time one who would abase the sovereignty of the Egyptians... were he reared to manhood... Alarmed thereat, the king, on the sage's advice, ordered that every male child born to the Israelites should be destroyed by being cast into the river.' At this juncture Amram's wife had conceived, and he was in great perplexity what to do. But God appeared to him in a dream, and told him, 'This child, whose birth has filled the Egyptians with such dread that they have condemned to destruction all the offspring of the Israelites, shall indeed be thine; he shall escape those who are watching to destroy him, and reared in marvellous wise, he shall deliver the Hebrew race from their bondage in Egypt.'[12]

Since with the Nativity records we are in the realm of historicised fable, neither *Matthew* nor *Luke* can serve as reliable authorities as to when and where Jesus was born. We will need to consider whether we can obtain assistance from other sources, especially whether it is practicable to determine the date when Jesus set out on his mission and approximately what his age was at this time. For this purpose the records relating to John the Baptist are obviously important, both canonical and uncanonical.

But we must not wholly throw overboard the significance of the legends of our two evangelists. Essentially they are Messianic, however dressed up in certain pagan trappings. Their concern is with the birth of a king of Israel, not a king of Angels, with God's son by adoption, not by essence,[13] with the ultimate hero of all the heroes of Hebrew antiquity. Let us by all means enjoy these tales as tributes to him, but keeping – as we should – within the Messianic terms of reference, and not confusing history and legend.

Notes and References

1. See *John* vii. 41-42, 52.
2. See above, p. 40.
3. Josephus, *Jewish Antiquities*, Bk. XVIII. 4. But this was in AD 6.
4. *Matt.* ii. 16, and see above, birth of John the Baptist.
5. See also pp. 73-74.
6. *Peake's Commentary on the Bible*, p. 701.
7. Cf. *John* viii. 57, "Thou art not yet fifty years old, and has Abraham seen thee?"
8. *Peake's Commentary*, p. 726. See also L. H. Feldman's note (a) to his translation of Josephus, *Antiq*. Bk. XVIII. 1 (*Loeb Classical Library*). This gives additional information negativing Ramsay's view.
9. The language leaves in no doubt that there had been no previous census.
10. Josephus, *Antiq*. Bk. XVIII. 1-4
11. See *Jewish Encycl*. under 'Abraham'.
12. Josephus, *Antiq*. Bk. II. 205-216.
13. *Luke* does not say Jesus is divine. He says: 'He shall *be called* son of the Highest; and the Lord shall give him the throne of his father David' (i. 32). This had been the position of Solomon.

11.

Unto Us a Child is born

The Gospels naturally make much of the birth of Jesus as heir to the throne of David, as the awaited Messiah. Their accounts of the event, as we have seen, are adorned with appropriate legends in the versions furnished by *Matthew* and *Luke*. They would appear to be unknown to the authors of *Mark* and *John*, and may have had their genesis as an outcome of early controversy about the Messiahship of Jesus. The differences in the two versions are such that no clear evidence emerges from them which throws light on both the date and the details relating to the Nativity, and they do not therefore contribute positively to our knowledge of Jesus when he began his public activities. But we do have some indirect evidence, and this can help us up to a point. Part of this relates to that extraordinary contemporary of Jesus, the prophet John the Baptist. His birth story also is largely legendary, but in his case there is a shade more of access to information governing his history. We have to do the best we can with the intimations from the available sources.

With what reliability we have no means of knowing, *Luke* claims that the mother of John and the mother of Jesus were related, and that their offspring were almost of an age, John being older by a few months. From *Luke* also we get a positive date for the beginning of the Baptist's ministry; and it can certainly be proposed that at this juncture John must have been a full-grown man.

So remarkable and Messianically significant was that event that *Luke* introduces it with a chronological flourish in terms that might have come from some written source of the Baptist sect.

Now in the fifteenth year of the reign of Tiberius Caesar, Pontius Pilate being governor of Judea, and Herod [i.e. Antipas] being tetrarch of Galilee, and his brother Philip tetrarch of Iturea and

76

of the region of Trachonitis, and Lysanias the tetrarch of Abilene, Annas and Caiaphas being the high priests, the word of
God came unto John the son of Zechariah in the wilderness. And
he came into all the country about Jordan, preaching the baptism
of repentance for the remission of sins. (*Luke* iii. 1-3)

The fifteenth year of Tiberius as emperor was AD 29, and this
date may well be correct for the beginning of the Baptist's ministry.
According to *Luke* he would then have been about twenty-four years
of age, with Jesus a few months younger. It is not stated in which
year Jesus was baptised by John, only that he was then approaching
thirty, which would be approximately correct for AD 34. The year
from September 33 to September 34 was a Jewish Sabbatical Year,
and this would seem to be reflected in the sermon of Jesus at Nazareth
shortly after his baptism, when he made reference to 'the acceptable
year of the Lord.'[1]

Very shortly after this John the Baptist was arrested by Herod
Antipas, and executed in AD 35. Josephus confirms this and relates
the circumstances. We may provisionally suggest, therefore, that Jesus
was crucified at the Passover of AD 36, when on *Luke*'s testimony
he would have been in his thirty-first year.

If we do not choose this we have an alternative, which would make
Jesus considerably older. The deduction we can make from *Matthew*'s
account in his Nativity story is that Jesus was born some two or three
years before the death of Herod the Great, which occurred in 4 BC.
If we say 7 BC for the birth of Jesus, then he would fully have reached
forty in AD 34, and in the course of his public activities it might be
said to him, as in *John* viii. 57, 'Thou art not yet fifty years old, and
hast thou seen Abraham?'

What is obvious is that both traditions cannot be right. They are
mutually exclusive.

As a guide to the probabilities let us here think of the family of
Jesus. It was quite a large family. *Matthew* gives the names of four
younger brothers of Jesus (xiii. 55-56) and indicates that he must
have had no fewer than two sisters. We must allow around ten years
for the arrival of these other six children after the birth of Jesus, and
this would fit in with what is stated in *Luke* (ii. 41-52) that Joseph
the father of Jesus was alive and by no means aged when the pil-
grimage to Jerusalem was made at the Passover when Jesus was
twelve years of age.

When Jesus began his public activities and visited Nazareth at a fairly early stage (*Mark* vi. 1-6, *Matt.* xiii. 54-58, *Luke* iv. 14-30)[2] the local people, surprised at the authority with which he spoke, exclaimed, 'Isn't he Joseph's son?' or 'Isn't he the carpenter's son?' The implication is that Jesus's father had not very long been deceased. And the reference to the sisters of Jesus may suggest that they were still unmarried. This would be likely enough if Jesus was then twenty-eight or twenty-nine, but unlikely if he was then about forty, seeing that Jewish girls usually married young.

The indications of the Gospel references are that at the time of Jesus's mission his immediate family was still a unit, living under one roof. The brothers and sisters of Jesus were not dispersed by having households of their own. In these circumstances a great responsibility rested upon the shoulders of Jesus as head of the family after his father's death, to care for his widowed mother and the younger children, and in due course the dowries of his sisters would have to be provided. It would be regarded as quite unnatural and reprehensible that Jesus should abandon his domestic responsibilities to become a travelling preacher.

The kindest interpretation that could be put upon the circumstances was that Jesus had gone out of his mind. The less charitable conclusion was that he was suffering from demon possession (*Mark* iii. 21-22). His mother and brothers *as a body* accordingly came to fetch him home. But Jesus refused to go with them on the grounds that he was now responsible for a much larger family. All who would do the will of God were now his mother and brothers and sisters (*Matt.* xii. 46-50, *Luke* viii. 19-21). There is clear acknowledgement here that Jesus was well aware of his family responsibilities. His mother and brothers act as a unit to get control of him, natural enough if he was around thirty. None of the circumstances would appear to suggest that at this time Jesus had turned forty.

This conclusion is reinforced by *John*'s Gospel where, apparently at this time, Jesus with his mother and brothers and disciples all go to Capernaum together (*John* ii. 12). The same Gospel conveys that his brothers remained in close contact with him; and even though in his lifetime they did not believe in him they felt fully entitled to proffer advice (*John* vii. 1-10). This would be natural enough for young men in their twenties, very positive in their ideas, with all the world before them and not yet settled down to a relatively humdrum existence. The way the brothers of Jesus advise him in *John*'s Gospel does not sound at all like persons of maturity counselling someone of forty-one years of age. They tell Jesus, 'Cross into Judea, that your disciples there too may see the miracles you perform. For no one does anything in secret if he seeks to be in the public eye. If you perform these miracles show yourself to the world.'

We are inclined in our imagination to think of Jesus and the Twelve as roughly in the age group twenty-five to thirty-five, especially in view of the subsequent travels of the Apostles for a great many years after the Crucifixion. We think of Peter as having been martyred in Rome around AD 65, being then in his late sixties. And we are probably right.

But tradition also tells us, and the historian Josephus confirms it, that James (Jacob), the next younger brother of Jesus, was martyred in AD 62, having acted as head of the Christian community for about a quarter of a century. After the fall of Jerusalem in AD 70 James was succeeded by Simeon son of Cleopas, who was his first cousin, and also, of course, a first cousin of Jesus. Simeon was credited with being a centenarian when he was martyred around AD 104 in the reign of Trajan.[3]

The information, as will be appreciated, has an importance in helping us to apprehend the personality and character of Jesus. When he takes the stage he is a man with an overriding commitment, a man who is already convinced that he is the Messiah of Israel. He has a remarkably clear idea of what he has to do and how to set about doing it. What has prepared him?

The Christian view of Jesus does not call for such a question; but we are moving on the plane of history and biography, not of theology, especially non-Jewish theology, where Jesus cannot be credited with superhuman knowledge and capacities or with personal perfection. He is a Jewish youth, living at a time of great suffering for his people; but also one of great spiritual excitement, with predictions flying around that the Climax of the Ages was near at hand, which would be confirmed by the appearance of the Messiah, who would be a descendant of King David. The Coming One's first task would be to gather together the faithful remnant of Israel and win back those who had fallen away, that through Israel the nations of the world should be redeemed.

In the time of Jesus there were still living a number of known descendants of the House of David, and his own family was among them. It would not, therefore, be surprising that he should be fired with the notion that it might be his destiny to be the awaited Messiah. His pious and proud father could well have been instrumental in stimulating such a conviction. The effect would be that the boy Jesus, cherishing the idea in his imagination, would be eager, without publicising it, to seek to inform himself about the Messiah's function.

He was a strange boy, but not so unusual in having a private life of his own. We have referred to the story, that when he was twelve, at the time the family was visiting Jerusalem at the Passover season, he went off by himself, without telling his parents, to put questions to the Jewish sages in the Temple. It seems to have been characteristic of him to act like this. When he began his campaign we have the account of his betaking himself to the wilderness to clarify his ideas of the Messiah's function, which must be divested of self-aggrandisement in any shape or form and wholly submissive to the will of God. Even when he had close disciples he would sometimes go off by himself, without telling them, or walk ahead of them wrapped in his own thoughts. His teaching on prayer stressed that it was an act of private devotion. We can believe, therefore, that it did not come easy for him to relate to other people, and more particularly to women, though they were attracted to him. And he was so extremely sensitive physically that he felt it if someone in a milling crowd touched him intentionally (*Mark* v. 27).

It has been suggested that Jesus was homosexual. That is to oversimplify, and to fail to appreciate the extreme solitariness of his Messianic status, and the further incapacity that he could not openly confess it. He did need human solace profoundly, and it was more appropriately available and acceptable in terms of his mission in male disciples with whom he could be at ease. There is no evidence whatever of his isolating himself from the opposite sex though matrimony could not figure in his programme.

As we have seen, Jesus could not be wrapped up in his family, and as the Messiah all Israel was his family. It is quite possible, therefore, that quite early, in what are called the Silent Years, prior to the visit of Jesus to the Jordan to be baptised by John, Jesus had left home for a protracted period to learn more of the Messianic Hope. We find him speaking in terms – for example in describing himself as the Son of Man[4] – which suggest that he had visited Essene camps in the wilderness. As they were a prophetic order with skill in healing, and deeply involved in Messianic matters, it would be natural for Jesus to communicate with them. But though he may have stayed with them for a time there is no evidence that he enrolled as a neophyte, as some writers have proposed. His Messianic function demanded a public life, not a retreat from it even for a worthy purpose. And as we have already stressed, Jesus saw it as a prime responsibility to seek for and save the lost sheep of the House of Israel. It was the sinners, not the righteous, who needed him.

The child is father of the man; but in the case of Jesus it is the personality of the man which tells us something about the child. We have noted how sensitive he was, with an inner life of his own which embraced imaginings regarding his own destiny. Evidently he was very bright and intelligent, with keen powers of observation. This can be judged by the stories he told, and the illustrations he used, almost entirely taken from real life in his own land. He was familiar with the contemporary social and political scene. But of the world in general outside the Land of Israel he knew almost nothing. He never overstepped its bounds, or entered any Gentile country, city or building. He was almost entirely unfamiliar with alien religions, history, geography and culture. His languages were Hebrew and Aramaic, with a smattering of Greek and Latin.

As a Jew Jesus knew his Bible intimately. And equally well he knew the prayers, praises, and religious practices of his people, centred both on the synagogue and the home. The so-called *Paternoster* recommended by Jesus to his disciples derives from Jewish daily prayers. It was customary for such a brief abstract to be used on journeys.

Evidently, and quite naturally because of his link with King David, Jesus had a particular love of the *Psalms*. His visits to Jerusalem had not been many, almost entirely confined to the celebration of the great Pilgrim Feasts, Passover, Pentecost and Tabernacles. He had seen with awe the glories of the Temple and listened to the chants of the Levitical choir. But he would have been brought up with little personal respect for the ruling chief priests, who had sold themselves to the Romans for personal power and gain. We know of him that he had a profound personal faith in a God who was very close to him and guiding his destiny. He would have enjoyed singing to the Lord, and he had – as his quoted speeches show – an aptitude for poetic composition.

At the same time there was something else about him, a creative and planning capacity which was to serve him in good stead as a skilful strategist in conducting his Messianic campaign.[5] In another age, and like many Jews, he could have been a master of chess.

By nature Jesus was, as we have seen, a rather reserved person, one reason perhaps why he was not very intimate with family and friends. But evidently he had adored his father, whom he had lost when he was at a very impressionable age. Thereafter he was dedicated to and caught up in his Messianic responsibilities, where his only father was God. And this was certified to him at the magical moment when the hairy hand of the Elijah-like figure of John the Baptist plunged him beneath the waters of the Jordan when the royal dignity of sonship of God was conferred upon him.

Notes and References

1. The painting by Gerbrand van den Eeckhout on the front cover of this book is also known as *Christ teaching in the Synagogue at Nazareth*, where these words were spoken by Jesus. (Publisher's note)
2. Ibid. Some art historians believe that particularly verses 20 and 21 from *Luke* iv are depicted in this picture. (Publisher's note)
3. Hegesippus, *Memoirs* (2nd century AD), quoted by Eusebius, *Ecclesiastical History*, iii. 32.
4. The Son of Man doctrine is prominent in the *Book of Enoch* and other Essene texts. And see below, Ch. 15.
5. I developed this theme in my book *The Passover Plot*.

12.

The Lie of the Land

There was a glory in the Great Adventure on which Jesus was now embarked, and also a gloom. At the outset the gloom was largely anaesthetised. It was a heady business to have been designated as Messianic son of God, and the story of the Temptation in the Wilderness conveys what were some of its perils. Fortunately faith, and a countryman's common sense, had prevailed, and the Tempter was put to flight. But with a heightened apprehension Jesus was now having to face the facts, the stark realities. And we have to face them too as I was to discover as I pursued my researches. The Christian image of a Divine Jesus walking the roads of Palestine, benignly healing and preaching in almost complete ignorance of contemporary circumstances, is not sustained by a careful study of the Gospels. The conferment of Messiahship meant that Jesus was put in a position not only of moral, but of political leadership. But how could the latter be exercised in a country that was now under the iron heel of Rome? Jesus was one individual, with neither material power nor prestige, having to pit his wits against one of the greatest organised forces the world had ever seen, and one, moreover, which was convinced of its own divine destiny.

We have a fair guide to conditions in the Land of Israel in the writings of Josephus, and we have more evidence from other available sources, so that there is no justification for the prejudiced and perverted representations all too frequently found in the works of writers in the Christian interest.

This is then the place to come to grips with reality, and view things as they really were in the time of Jesus.

The Jewish homeland was not a large country. One could travel from end to end of it in a few days. It had a longish seaboard on the west, but with few seaports of consequence, like Caesarea, Joppa and Ascalon, and these with substantial non-Jewish populations. When Judea came under direct Roman government in AD 6 Caesarea became the principal place of residence of the Roman procurator, who was a glorified imposts collector and immediately responsible to the Roman legate for Syria with his seat at Antioch. There was access to other ports, like Sidon, Tyre and Ptolemais, but his Phoenician territory was part of Roman Syria.

The Jewish lands in the time of Jesus were no longer under single government as they had been under Herod the Great. They had been divided among his heirs. Archelaus had received Judea and Samaria, but because of his tyrannical rule he was deposed by the Romans in AD 6, and a Roman governor was installed. Galilee with Perea on the east of the Jordan came under Herod Antipas, while the outlying northern territories of Gaulanitis, Trachonitis, Auranitis and Batanea had been assigned to Herod Philip. With direct Roman rule in Judea, Samaria received a measure of self-government, but not independence.

The effect of these circumstances was that Jewish unity had substantially been destroyed, making common action almost impossible, and facilitating Roman control over the whole country. It was not unlike the situation of some European countries under the Nazis during the Second World War.

Conditions were worsened by the Roman continuation and expansion of repressive policies which had been instituted by Herod the Great to keep his subjects in order. Political freedom had virtually been abolished, and the assembly of crowds was considered to be dangerously subversive. Spies and informers abounded seeking to catch words from Jewish speakers which could be interpreted as treasonable. What Christian thinks of this when quoting the Sermon on the Mount? The periodical Roman tax had been imposed, and brutal Roman mercenaries were at hand to seize goods, especially of the poor, and to quell resistance. Some of the soldiery were very willing to rob and to inflict penalties to supplement their low pay. Many Jews were driven to become bandits and freedom fighters, carrying out raids and holding rich victims to ransom. All over the country the crosses upon which men had cruelly died bore witness to a nation cowed but not subdued.

Satan was in the ascendant, whom they called Belial, grinding the faces of the poor, inflicting diseases, especially those which were the result of poverty and affliction, madness and nervous disorders.

He also sat in the seats of power with certain Jewish chief priests as tacitly his worshippers, great families like those of Annas and Boethus.

Not unlike modern Israel the Jewish lands in the times of Jesus were surrounded by Gentile areas, Syrian, Arab and Greek, alien in religion and inclined to be hostile. To the north and on the coast lay Syria, embracing Phoenicia. On the east were Nabataean and Arab lands, with the Greeks of the Decapolis (Ten Towns). In the south were the Idumeans, while in the centre no love was lost between Samaritans and Jews, and Samaria served very effectively to restrict fraternal relationships between Galileans and Judeans.

Confronted with all these circumstances who would wish to be the Messiah, king of all Israel? Most Christian authors of a Life of Jesus, and some Jewish ones, do not dwell on the political difficulties of his situation, especially if, according to prophecy, he was required to meet them without force of arms. Many choose to ignore that his status was political, treating him purely as a religious figure, and with Christians even more, as Deity incarnate, something wholly alien to Jesus's own Jewish faith. The Gospels do not obliterate the social and political conditions, though they do not stress them, since they were not Jewish royalists and were appealing mainly to non-Jews in the cities of the Roman Empire. The Romans were not fools, and they were well aware that what the Christians were teaching was hostile and subversive, even – as was not always the case[1] – when the followers of Jesus were very careful and circumspect. That is why the Romans refused to license Christianity as a religious cult.

It would be asking altogether too much of the Evangelists to require that they should deliberately draw attention to matters which would furnish their adversaries with ammunition. The full story of Jesus, should it be made known, would convict the Christians out of their own mouths. As it was, the Evangelists were already removed a considerable distance from the reality, and it was not too difficult for them to concentrate on the moral and spiritual teaching of Jesus, which already existed in a collected form.[2] The remarkable thing is how much of the Messianic and Jewish was still represented in the Gospels, because of their dependence on underlying sources.

But our concern just now is with how Jesus, substantially aware of the problems confronting him, was proposing to overcome them. His primary Messianic function was to bring his people back to God, so that they would be qualified to be a Light to the Gentiles, and the instruments of the world's salvation. For this they needed healing in soul and body. There had to be time to acquire and instruct envoys, opportunity to preach and to teach, to conduct a Messianic campaign under the most difficult conditions, which would not be stifled and abruptly terminated by the forces in control of the country. He himself, with God's guidance, had to contrive to remain alive and at liberty.

The authors of the Synoptic Gospels, with little, if any, awareness of the significance of what they were stating, materially assist us in revealing Jesus's plan of campaign. Following his baptism, he had begun his activities a few months before a Jewish Sabbatical Year, falling in the period AD 33-34.[3] In this year, when there was a very substantial reduction of agricultural activities, many thousands of people would not be working and were free to move around. The year 34-35 was a Roman Census year, which itself involved some movement of the population. With multitudes idle, and on the road, the resources on the authorities would be stretched, and they could not be nearly so vigilant in preventing crowds assembling. And further, these events themselves encouraged in the people thoughts of liberty linked with the Messianic Hope.

There was another factor at this particular period which told further in favour of Jesus, while at the same time warning him to be very circumspect. The ruler of Galilee, Herod Antipas, had married Herodias, wife of his half-brother, and his own wife, daughter of the Nabataean King Harith (Aretas), had fled to her father, who declared war on Antipas. John the Baptist, who at this time had been drawing large crowds, denounced Antipas publicly; and the monarch had every reason to fear that there might be a revolt of his subjects when he took the majority of his troops out of the country to fight the Nabataeans. He therefore had John arrested and took him with him to the frontier fortress of Machaerus.[4] There subsequently, as the story goes (*Mark* vi.17-28), when Antipas's anniversary celebrations were held, the prophet was beheaded at the instigation of Herodias.

Thus, when Jesus began his public ministry in Galilee, the people had more freedom of movement by reason of the Sabbatical Year, and owing to the war with Harith there was much less supervision. The thoughts of the Galileans had already been directed by the prophet to freedom and the imminent advent of the Kingdom of God on earth. All this added up for Jesus to a sign from Heaven.

But the propitious circumstances, as I have pointed out, did not convey to Jesus that he might throw caution to the winds. Consequently he did not initially give any hint that he was the Messiah, and simply took up the Baptist's call to repentance. Had he done otherwise his activities would speedily have terminated. It needs to be stressed again what Christian expositors have failed to do, that where Rome ruled under the imperial regime it was a capital crime to claim to be king without the sanction of Caesar. If Jesus, therefore, had presented himself as the *Christ*, as the king of the Jews, he would immediately have been seized and executed.[5] In the end that was the crime under Roman law, not Jewish law, for which he suffered. His cross carried particulars of his crime: 'This is Jesus, King of the Jews.' He had violated the emperor's majesty, and since Caesar was deemed divine that was also in those days blasphemy. It is on Roman record that a man was even executed for changing his clothes in front of the emperor's statue.

For almost the whole of his public life not only would Jesus not refer to himself as Messiah, if we follow the Synoptic Gospels, he would not allow anyone else, human or demon, to address him as such. He immediately silenced them. Instead he cloaked himself in anonymity, only penetrable by those 'on the inside' like the secretive Essenes, by referring to himself as the Son of Man, a term having Messianic connotations for these mystics. The circumstance has been seized upon quite wrongly by exegetes wishing to establish that Jesus did not claim to be the Jewish Messiah. They have quite failed to appreciate why Jesus was so circumspect.

In his public speeches Jesus necessarily had to teach about the advent of the Kingdom of God, and the word Kingdom obviously had its dangers. Accordingly Jesus cleverly used the device of parables, moral tales, to cloak his message, so that the purport could not be used against him by spies and informers in the crowds. He signalled his intention with the words, 'He that hath ears to hear, let him hear.' We also read (*Mark* iv. 10-12):

> And when he was alone, they that were about him with the Twelve asked of him the parable. And he said unto them, Unto you it is given to know the secret of the Kingdom of God: but *unto them that are outside* all these things are done in parables: that 'seeing they may see, and not perceive; and hearing they may hear, and not understand.'[6]

Only when Jesus reached the climax of his activities, and purposefully directed his steps towards Jerusalem, did he openly and deliberately reveal himself as the Messiah, knowing full well what the consequences must be. First of all he prepared his immediate disciples when they were in the area of Caesarea Philippi by asking them, 'Whom do men say that I am?' Apparently he was regarded simply as a prophet in one guise or another. He then challenged them, 'And you, who do you say that I am?' It was Peter who burst out, 'You are the Messiah.' Jesus agreed, and praised Peter for the insight God had given him, but he admonished his disciples not to disclose his true identity (*Mark* viii. 27-33).

It was at Jericho on the way to Jerusalem for the Passover that things began to change. Here a blind man called Bar-Timaeus, hearing that Jesus was passing by, cried out, 'Jesus, Son of David, pity me!' Many told him to be silent, making such a dangerous utterance. But this time Jesus did not support them: he accepted the royal designation.

From this moment, as it seemed, discretion was thrown to the winds. But in reality from this point Jesus was putting into effect plans which he had formulated well in advance and had secured the co-operation of well-placed trusted friends. No longer was his Messianic status to be obscured: King of Israel he was, and to be acknowledged as such by his people, knowing full well that he was defying the sovereignty of Caesar in the name of the God of Israel.

From this moment both the followers of Jesus and the pilgrim crowd were geared up to expect they knew not what. Neither were they disappointed. At the approach to Bethphage and Bethany, east of the Mount of Olives and Jerusalem, Jesus sent two of his disciples to fetch an ass's colt, which he had arranged with his Bethany friends to be on hand. When it was brought Jesus mounted the beast, an act which was seen as the fulfilment of the prediction of the Prophet Zechariah: 'Rejoice greatly, O daughter of Zion; shout, O daughter of Jerusalem: behold, thy King cometh unto thee: he is just, and having salvation; lowly, and riding upon an ass, even upon a colt the foal of an ass' (*Zech*. ix. 9).

Immediately there was an excited uproar. Jesus had acknowledged himself as king. People ran to strew his path with foliage, and even with their garments, as they resumed the journey to Jerusalem. Those in front of Jesus and those behind took up the chant: '*Hosanna!* [Save now!] Blessed is he that cometh in the name of the Lord. Blessed be the kingdom of our father David, that cometh in the name of the

Lord.' As Jerusalem came into view from the Mount of Olives, crowned with the glorious Temple, Jesus was overcome with emotion and wept. *John* states that the people poured out of the city to greet him. It was his moment of triumph. To those who were alarmed at what was happening and the plaudits of the Jewish populace, fearing an uprising followed by a Roman massacre, Jesus cried, 'If they should be silent, the very stones will call out.'

We learn that Jesus went into the Temple either the same or the following day and boldly attacked the hucksters there in scathing terms. The Temple market was operated by the chief priests who profited from the sale of sacrificial beasts and birds and the exchange of heathen currency for the Jewish shekel. The Pharisees called it Annas's Bazaar. It was a deliberate action by Jesus, which would have popular acclaim, as well as provoking the lordly chief priests who were Rome's agents.

Jesus was not ignorant of what would be the outcome of what he was doing. But he was not in immediate danger, since the authorities were not yet clear whether he was claiming to be king or prophet, and they needed to be wary at the inflammable season of the Passover not to provoke a Jewish uprising.

But Jesus had wisely taken his own precautions. He moved in Jerusalem only in the midst of a patriotic Galilean multitude, and he did not spend one night in the city. Every evening before the city gates were closed he left for Bethany, attended by his sturdy disciples, so that he could not readily be either arrested or assassinated. Between him and the government forces were the myriad tents of Jewish pilgrims packed round the city for the festival, who at this season could find no lodging in the capital. Jesus, therefore, would have ample warning of any armed force sent against him.

The Passover was an excitable patriotic occasion for the Jews, when they could readily be aroused to militant action, especially if Roman troops were not judiciously kept in their quarters. Pontius Pilate had had every reason to know from experience how fanatically rebellious the Jews could be when their national and religious feelings were flouted. Evidently only recently there had been an outbreak in the city in which a certain Jesus bar-Abba (Barabbas) and his associates had been involved, and they were now in custody awaiting sentence.

To get the true picture we have carefully to read the Biblical Gospels alongside the works of the Jewish historian Josephus, and delve into all the available records.

The skilful planning of Jesus enabled him to keep the Passover in Jerusalem with the Twelve. He had made secret prior arrangements with one on whom he could wholly depend, probably the previous winter when he had been in Jerusalem at the season of Chanukah, the Jewish feast of Dedication, as *John* relates. The man whom he trusted with his life appears to have had a substantial house on Mount Zion.[7] When his disciples – his most intimate disciples Peter and John – asked Jesus where he would hold the Passover *Seder*, he did not even to them furnish any name and address. Instead he told them to go into the city, where at a certain place (possibly the Pool of Siloam) they would encounter a man carrying a water-pot. They were to follow him, and he would lead them to a certain house. There they were to ask a certain question, and would then be shown a large upper room where they could prepare.

The Gospel record has all the ingredients of a fictional thriller when we come to examine it carefully. But there is no reason to doubt its substantial accuracy. Jesus had been quite sure at Bethany, and perhaps much earlier, that he would be betrayed to the authorities, and by whom, as his words to Judas Iscariot indicate, 'What you have to do, do quickly' (*John* xiii. 27). There is strong suspicion here that Jesus and Judas were in collusion. But Jesus had seen to it that his host and household in Jerusalem were not involved. The arrest would be made late at night outside the city in the Garden of Gethsemane in the Kidron Valley on the east. And those who came to take Jesus were not Roman troops, when there might have been a fight: they were the Temple police and other forces under the control of the High Priest and Sanhedrin, acting on information received. We learn here that some of the disciples of Jesus were armed, including Peter. But Jesus stopped them interfering with his arrest.

The whole scenario answers to the conditions prevailing at the time, as we are able to learn about them. And they present us with a Jesus who is not at all the God of Christian doctrine. He is a man of parts, a born leader and organiser, with strong feelings, and indeed highly sensitive physically and emotionally. He is able to plan and weigh his moves to bring about the desired results, and with a remarkable sense of timing. To achieve his ends he is fully prepared to enlist the co-operation of people, and evidently, as we learn, he had in Judea several influential friends on whose help he could rely.

The obstacles in the way of this Galilean artisan, the magnitude of the organised forces ranged against him, were tremendous. But with faith in his God, with the blood of kings in his veins, with a courageous heart and a creative mind, he was to prove equal to the challenge. The great pity is that the Church was to deprive itself of the capacity to recognise his human worth and mental processes.

NOTES AND REFERENCES

1. Compare the *Book of Revelation*.
2. See next chapter, p.98.
3. See Schonfield, *The Pentecost Revolution*, and p.77 above.
4. On the arrest of John see Josephus, *Antiquities*, Bk. XVIII. 116-119.
5. See Schonfield, *The Passover Plot*.
6. See also *Luke* xx. 19-20.
7. See Schonfield, *The Pentecost Revolution*.

13.

The Gospels as Sources

The man the Synoptic Gospels disclose was very evidently no 'Gentle Jesus meek and mild'. Neither was he the arrogant and largely alien (Gentile) Christ of much of the Fourth Gospel, who far from concealing his identity readily presents himself as God's son and spokesman, and in language which alienates him from his people and religion. *John*'s Gospel is in part Hellenic metaphysics, though it contains a good deal that is of biographical value. There are some elements which are strongly Essene and also convey that the writer has personal knowledge and inside information, and these have led some scholars to treat this Gospel as the earliest of the canonical Gospels. We have to investigate this circumstance, and the origin of the other three Gospels, to determine their worth as authorities.

It may have seemed to be putting the cart before the horse to have been treating of the activities of Jesus before considering the reliability of the Gospels as sources of information. But I felt it was necessary to illustrate that the Gospels convey more about Jesus, often unwittingly and incidentally, than is conveyed to those who read them for religious guidance and inspiration.

The Gospels, with the possible exception of *Luke*, were not designed as historical biographies, though they were relating the story of Jesus in a fashion having some resemblance to Plutarch's *Lives of Great Men* written around the same period. Essentially, however, the Gospels still represented the announcement of the Good News that the awaited Messiah of the Jews had manifested himself. Incidentally, they could refer to matters which the authors either could not, or saw no need to, explain. They happened, but they had no particular bearing on the message of salvation.

Here are some examples. Jesus is informed about the Galileans 'whose blood Pilate had mingled with their sacrifices' (*Luke* xiii. 1).

This was a major incident of historical importance, and it is left in the air. A similar unexplained reference occurs in relation to the trial of Jesus, where in *Luke*'s version the Galilean ruler Herod Antipas is involved as well as Pontius Pilate. We read: 'And the same day Pilate and Herod were made friends together: for before they were at enmity between themselves.' (*Luke* xxiii. 12). Why had they been at enmity? Was it because of the massacre of Galileans, who were Herod's subjects, to which reference had been made earlier? Associated with that reference Jesus himself alludes to the death of eighteen persons at Jerusalem on whom 'the tower at Siloam fell, and slew them.' Again, when, and in what circumstances? From *Mark* we learn that at the time of the trial of Jesus, 'there was one named Bar-Abbas, who lay bound with them that had made insurrection with him, who had committed murder in the insurrection' (*Mark* xv. 7). What insurrection? This is a circumstance of major importance; but it is not elucidated.

Relevant, but of less consequence, is the allusion to otherwise unknown individuals. *Luke* speaks of certain women cured by Jesus. One was Joanna, the wife of Chuza, Herod's steward. Another was Susanna. Who was she? (*Luke* viii. 3) Simon of Cyrene carried the cross on which Jesus was to suffer. But peculiarly in *Mark* (xv. 21) he is referred to as the father of Alexander and Rufus. Are we to understand that Susanna, Alexander and Rufus became members of the Christian community? Otherwise why mention them in documents designed for readers outside Palestine to whom the names would have no significance? What such references suggest is the dependence of the Gospel writers on earlier sources to which they adhere with considerable faithfulness.

Christians are accustomed to treating the Gospels as totally dependable, as the very Word of God. The contradictions and inconsistencies do not readily strike them. Accordingly, they will accept as genuine various speeches put into the mouth of Jesus in circumstances where no record could have been made, or where exact recollection long after – especially of long discourses – would be virtually impossible. If we are concerned to be realistic we are compelled to approach these documents as belonging to their period, where the author's composition of speeches for leading personalities was taken for granted. There are many instances. Sometimes the intention of the author might be sectarian or dogmatic; but commonly the aim was to voice appropriate sentiments and increase dramatic effect.

As a typical illustration we may take the account given by Josephus of the last stand of the Jewish Zealots at Masada, after the fall of Jerusalem in AD 70. The night before the fortress was captured by the Romans the Jewish commander Eleazar addresses the survivors, recommending that they commit suicide rather than fall into the hands of the enemy. The speech, quite a considerable one, is given in full by Josephus, who of course was not present, and in terms that express what he deemed appropriate sentiments. Josephus goes on to relate how the advice of Eleazar was accepted and the whole garrison died to a man, killing one another after killing their families. The last left alive killed himself. The only survivors were an aged woman and five small children who had hidden themselves.[1] So who preserved the text of Eleazar's speech and communicated it subsequently to Josephus?

Similarly in the Gospels we are told of the terms in which Jesus prayed in the Garden of Gethsemane. It is a deeply moving story, heightened in *Luke* by the appearance of an angel. Yet it is made evident in the narration that no one could have heard the words of Jesus's prayers. He had removed himself at some distance from his disciples, and they had fallen asleep. We would not wish to lose such a poignant episode; but we have to appreciate that the words put into the mouth of Jesus were what was thought fitting.

It was customary to drink at least four cups of wine at the *seder*, the Passover supper, and moreover, as we have noted, the disciples were weary with sorrow as well. Yet we are invited by *John*'s Gospel to accept that, at the end of the service and the meal, Jesus made a very long speech to his disciples (occupying two whole chapters of the Biblical text), and that drowsy and dull of hearing as they were by this time the complete discourse as uniquely related in *John*'s Gospel (xiv-xv), was remembered and preserved verbatim to be put in a book more than half a century later.

When we examine this discourse attributed to Jesus, and some other speeches of his in this Gospel, we can see how unlike they are to the way Jesus expresses himself in the other Gospels. It is not the same man who is speaking, and moreover it is someone who is not a Jew as Jesus was. Addressing Jewish audiences he refers to '*your* fathers' instead of '*our* fathers' (*John* vi. 49), and to '*your* Law' instead of '*our* Law' (viii. 17). He even employs the language of alien cults in the passage which begins: 'Except ye chew the flesh of the Son of Man, and drink his blood, ye have no life in you.' (vi. 53) Very naturally, if they had heard such language, 'many of his disciples went back, and walked no more with him' (vi. 66).

When we study the Greek we can detect that the way in which Jesus holds forth in *John*'s Gospel, and the kind of sentiments he expresses, are characteristic of the writer of the *Epistles of John*, who describes himself not as Apostle but as Elder or Presbyter. There is something of a mystery here which I had to unravel in the researches preparatory to making my translation of the New Testament from the Greek.[2]

As some of my readers may know, I found most of the extant versions so influenced by the Church's doctrines after it had blossomed into the religion of Christianity, and down to the present day, that sometimes interpretation of the text had crept in. An objective and informed approach was demanded, as with other comparable documents of antiquity such as the Jewish Apocalyptic Writings, so ably treated by Christian scholars. In the end I had to edit and translate the whole of the New Testament with explanatory notes and references, since even the most modern versions suffered from incorrect rendering mainly due to lack of competence in Jewish matters. I am glad to say that my achievement was welcomed and applauded to a much greater extend that I had anticipated.

I was to learn a great deal from this experience, which necessarily involved delving into the traditions relating to the origins of the Gospels, their authorship and sources. It is unfortunate that these matters are almost completely concealed from the Christian layman, and very largely so from the clergy.

The very fact that the canonical Gospels were composed in Greek, the *lingua franca* of the Roman Empire, conveys that they were designed for the use of non-Jewish or mixed Hellenic Jewish and Gentile Christian communities in various parts of the Roman Empire bordering the Mediterranean.[3] Thus they are not the most primitive of the accounts of Jesus, and their form illustrates an accommodation both to the requirements and the literary fashions of the societies for which they were intended. Further, on the whole, they are guarded documents, very careful to present Jesus more prominently as teacher and healer and in varying degrees to convey his divinity. This was advisable, since in the period when the Gospels were written Christianity was not a religion licensed by the Roman authorities. It was regarded as a dangerous and subversive ideology, having its roots in a Jewish Messianism which had provoked the Jewish War of AD 66-

70 against the Romans, a rebellion that was still being fostered by underground plots and activities.

The remarkable thing is how much of Jewish nationalism and political Messianism was still detectable. It simply could not be eradicated without abandoning historicity and fundamental convictions deriving from the primitive sources available. This is both helpful and reassuring.

We know that a great many Gospels were extant, and the canonical ones would seem to have had several things to commend them. They were among the least extravagant in their contents. They had some traditional links with representative persons of note. They were also representative of the mainstream of Christian development and expression, and thus assisted Church unity. But they are not themselves contemporary documents. Between them and the time of Jesus several decades intervene, decades fraught with great change in Christian and Jewish circumstances. As to origin of the Greek texts, the probabilities – taking note of traditions – favour Egypt for *Matthew*, Italy for *Mark*, Greece for *Luke*, and Asia Minor for *John*.

We owe to Irenaeus in the late second century the fancy that the Gospels could not be more or fewer than four, since the world is divided into four zones and there are four principal winds. Moreover, the celestial Cherubim had four faces, like a lion, like a calf, like a man, and like an eagle (cf. *Rev*. iv. 6-8).[4] He omits to associate the choice with the Roman imperial rule of the lands north, south, east and west of the Mediterranean. Certain early traditions have been preserved throwing some light on how the canonical Gospels originated, and why the names they bear came to be associated with them. These traditions are certainly of value, but they do not eliminate the need to use our Gospels as authoritative with much greater caution than has been customary in ecclesiastical circles, especially where un-Jewish matters intruded.

It has to be faced that one could not have a fusion of Jewish and Gentile concepts without to an extent compromising both. The result could only be a portrayal of Jesus which was a hybrid, the degree having some dependence on the region in which the Gospel was composed. In the last resort there could be no compatibility of a human Jewish Messiah, graced by *adoption* with 'the divinity that doth hedge a king', and an individual credited with being Deity Incarnate, simultaneously both God and Man. Jewish idiom often used the expression 'flesh and blood' to signify a human being having

96

mortality. Deity being pure Spirit could not be so described. The conjunction proposed by Christianity, particularly in the Fourth Gospel and in *I. John* iv. 3, was an impossibility. A celestial being wearing the *appearance* of humanity might be credible, the position adopted by the Docetists that Jesus only *seemed* to be a man.

We have to come down heavily on the side of the humanity of Jesus, which has historical precedence and is also realistic. That is, of course, if we regard deity as representing perfection, which the Greeks did not. In the Gospels Jesus exhibits very positive human traits and feelings. He often expresses quite ungodlike sentiments and exhibits quite ungodlike behaviour. For the historian, therefore, the choice is not difficult. The pagan theistic interpretations have to be set aside as understandable but not factual.

But there is something more, which should have weighed with Christian divines more than it appears to have done. Jesus was a sincere and practising Jew, reared on the unequivocal distinction between God and any terrestrial form or substance. The many thousands of followers of Jesus in Israel headed by Jacob (James) his younger brother, continued to be staunch Jews (*Acts* xxi. 18-24). They had no notion of Jesus as incarnate Deity. And among them were Peter and nearly all the Twelve Apostles who had been the companions of Jesus. Among them also were his mother and several close relations. The nearest we get to an exalted, but not divine, status is an echo of the Gospel Transfiguration story in the late pseudo-Petrine document *II. Peter* i. 16-18, and even there more reliance is based on Old Testament prophecy, as also in *I. Peter* ii. 22-24, where the description of Christ's sufferings is given largely in the language of the Suffering Servant in *Isaiah*.

The Apostle Paul gained his knowledge of Jesus from Peter and the others at Jerusalem; but the activities of Jesus are hardly mentioned in his epistles, though he did know that he was a descendant of King David (*Rom.* i. 3). He also knew that Jesus was not God, and plainly stated to Timothy, 'There is One God, and one mediator between God and man, the *man* Christ Jesus.' Paul also tells Timothy of the good and noble confession that Jesus made before Pontius Pilate (*I. Tim.* vi. 13). We do not know what this was, since in our Gospels he was either silent, or vacillating and non-committal. Of all the sayings of Jesus which Paul might have quoted the only one he does cite is not in the Gospels at all (*Acts* xx. 35).

As a consequence of the Jewish War with the Romans (AD 66-70) any substantial communication between the followers of Jesus in Palestine and those in western lands was effectively destroyed. Multitudes of his Jewish disciples perished in the war. Some managed to flee to Egypt and to the east. The most coherent body of which we learn much later found asylum in the north-east under the leadership of a first cousin of Jesus, Simeon son of Cleopas, who survived until the reign of the Emperor Trajan. Thus in the crucial period for Christianity in various lands round the Mediterranean when our four Gospels were produced there was little direct access to primitive Hebrew and Aramaic sources of information. The Church at large was mainly dependent on such information, oral and written, as had reached the west before the war.

Among oral sources had been the invaluable addresses given by Peter, which tradition claims to have been the basis of the *Gospel of Mark*; and the personal reminiscences in old age of John the Priest at Ephesus were made available at the very close of the century.

But we also learn of certain written sources, two in particular. One type consisted of passages from the Old Testament, and perhaps some uncanonical books, held to relate to the Messiah with illustrations of their fulfilment in Jesus. The other type contained collections of sayings of Jesus like those found at Oxyrhynchus ascribed to Judas Thomas, and in fuller form in Coptic at Nag-Hammadi. We may refer to these as the *Testimony Gospel* and the *Teaching Gospel*. They were originally written in Hebrew, and in the *Acts of Barnabas* their composition was attributed to Matthew.[5] They were quite short books, easily carried by the first Apostle. When translated, of course, they could become subject to changes and additions. Our present *Matthew* and *Luke*, the former especially, and to an extent *Mark*, give evidence of access to these sources, which helps to account for the persistence of strong Hebraic elements in their contents.

The partial preservation in the Gospels of such early material gives us confidence that substantially we are not denied access to the real Jesus. But we have to exercise great care in seeking to extract such material, since we do not have the primitive records at command and the manuscripts are chiefly those of Nicene Christianity. Where there is expansion of sayings or adaptation for Gentile Church requirements, or where anti-Jewish doctrine is introduced, we have to be ready to treat these elements as accommodation to external circumstances. What we must be thankful for is that our canonical Gospels retain so much that was contrary to a Gentile presentation of Jesus. From the remains of several uncanonical Gospels we can see how far many in the Early Church were prepared to go to rid themselves of the human and Jewish Jesus. They have their counterparts today in a number of Christian divines and theologians.

But Jesus without the King of the Jews is like Hamlet without the Prince of Denmark. The Christian has to dismount from his heathen hobby-horse, and become identified with the Messianism reflected in the name he bears, if he sincerely wishes to reach the Jesus of history.

NOTES AND REFERENCES

1. Josephus, *Jewish War*, vii. 323-326 and 342-388.
2. First published as *The Authentic New Testament* (Dobson Books, 1955); revised edition published as *The Original New Testament* in 1985 (Element Books).
3. Translations are usually furnished of Hebrew and Aramaic words cited in Greek spelling, and Jewish customs and practices are normally explained.
4. Irenaeus, *Against Heresies*, Bk. III. 8.
5. In the *Acts of Barnabas* they are referred to as (i) 'a book of the Word of God' and (ii) 'a narrative of miracles and doctrines'.

14.

The Fifth Gospel

The more I studied the canonical records the more conscious I became of the necessity to get behind them, to learn as much as possible of the history and ideas of the Jewish followers of Jesus. *The Acts of the Apostles* related some things about them, but almost entirely as a preface and background to the communication of the Messianic message to the Gentiles throughout the Roman Empire. The author was anxious to lend support and authority to Paul's position as the odd man out and as apostle to the Gentiles. Consequently he acknowledges and pays respect to the authoritative status of the Jewish followers of Jesus under their apostolic government at Jerusalem headed by no less a person than Jacob (James) the brother of Jesus. And he was at pains to tone down the conflict over the status of Gentile converts which suggested that Paul had been opposed and discredited by the parent body best qualified to represent Jesus.

But when the Church became predominantly non-Jewish it was anxious to remove itself altogether from a Jewish environment and go its separate way. This, however, it found it could not do if it was to maintain a relationship with the historical Jesus, whose Second Advent was still anticipated. When the Roman Empire came to terms with Christianity in the fourth century and adopted it as the official religion, the historical Jesus was very much brought back into the picture. Previously, Rome had been destroying all Christian records, and was now seeking to recover both sites in the Holy Land and relics relating to Jesus, and also information about the Early Church. This necessarily included the fortunes of the Jewish followers of Jesus. One outcome was the *Ecclesiastical History* composed by Eusebius of Caesarea. He was able to draw on more sources than we can today, since books were extant then which are not now available. Among them were the memoirs of the second-century writer Hegesippus in which much about the fortunes of the Jewish followers of Jesus was related from living memory.

But also in the fourth century there still flourished under names such as Nazoreans and Ebionites numerous communities in the Near East of Jewish followers of Jesus, possessing Hebrew and Aramaic Gospels. They attracted the particular interest of Jerome and Epiphanius. As a result we have access to additional Jesus sayings and traditions, and to material relating to the history and beliefs of the Jewish Christians in the Holy Land before and after the fall of Jerusalem in AD 70. These supplement, and also help to correct, the image represented by the canonical *Acts*.

It is to the great credit of Eusebius that in the Essenes of Egypt, known as Therapeuts and described by Philo of Alexandria, he recognised such a strong likeness to the primitive Christians that he supposed them to be one and the same. They were not, of course, identical; but honest investigation, especially since the discovery of the Dead Sea Scrolls, has revealed that there was greater dependence of the first followers of Jesus on Essene ideas, literature and organisation than the Church has been willing to admit.[1] And since we are told in the *Acts* that 'a great company of the priests were obedient to the faith' (*Acts* vi. 7), and many of them favoured the Essenes, and we also find Essene literature treated by the Christians as Scripture, such as the *Book of Enoch* (*Jude* 14-15; *I. Pet.* iii. 19-20[2]), there was some evidence even before the Scrolls came to light.

We now know that the Essenes were parties to a New Covenant (New Testament), and described themselves as 'the Poor' (*Ebionim*), and that their principal festival was Pentecost. They were also organised in communities under officers corresponding to bishops and deacons, and had a supreme council like the Christians. They had a mystical Messianic doctrine centred on a Son of Man. Indeed, the pattern of Christian structure and teaching represented in the *Acts of the Apostles* was ready-made among the Essenes. The Jewish followers of Jesus did not have to invent it. And being humble artisans as regards the Twelve, they probably could not have done so.

There is still a mystery about the relationship between the Nazoreans and Ebionites and the Essenes in their northern communities. Why did Saul of Tarsus journey particularly to Damascus to arrest there 'any of this Way' (*Acts* ix. 2)? And to what body did Ananias of Damascus belong? And we may ask, why before the siege of

Jerusalem did the Jewish followers of Jesus emigrate to the north-east? It is not at all surprising that at least one Jewish scholar, J.L. Teicher,[3] reached the conclusion that the Dead Sea Scrolls were documents of the early Jewish Christians.

The Jewish followers of Jesus in Israel were no negligible body. They were well organised under a council whose president was Jacob (James) the brother of Jesus, someone who had known him well. They informed Paul that there were *myriads* (ten thousands) of Jewish believers in Jesus as Messiah (*Acts* xxi. 20), and they remained wholly within Judaism. Therefore before we are entitled to comment on the Greek Gospels, which were relatively late compositions, it is surely our business to study with the greatest care such remains as have survived of the primitive Jewish followers of Jesus.

Why, we may ask, have the vast majority of Christians been most reluctant to explore the Jewish origins of Christianity, and the fortunes of the Jewish Apostolic Church? Surely such a quest should be a top priority for those who genuinely seek to inform themselves of what Jesus taught and represented, and thus how he was regarded by his native Jewish followers. From what we have noted above it is already clear that nothing that Jesus said or taught was alien to the tenets and practices of Judaism, or he would not have been able to enlist such a very large and conservative body of Jewish adherents. And this already casts grave doubts on the positions Jesus takes in *John*'s Gospel, and in certain places in the Synoptics (*Mark, Matthew* and *Luke*). We have therefore to be very circumspect as to how we employ them, and we are bound to take cognisance of certain things we find in the Fifth Gospel,[4] the remains of the *Gospel of the Hebrews*.

Many of my readers will never have heard of the existence of such a Gospel though what is known of its contents has been published, and I myself devoted a book to its investigation.[5] The Hebrew Gospel, as we would expect, was closest to *Matthew*, with certain agreements with readings in *Luke*. But it also had elements peculiar to itself, and its own version of incidents and sayings of Jesus. In the fourth century two types of the Gospel were known, one in use by the main body of Jewish followers of Jesus, the Nazoreans, and the other by the more eccentric Ebionites. The first type was translated into Latin by Jerome; but no copy of this version has been found. However, in his writings he gives a number of quotations, and in certain Gospel manuscripts the text of *Matthew* has marginal notes citing differences in 'the Jewish'. I was able to discover that a rabbinical parody known as the *Toldoth Jeshu* was based on the Hebrew Gospel and assisted in recovering its structure.

The Hebrew Gospel is important because in some cases it gives sayings and incidents more accurately than the Greek, and because it also illustrates – especially in the Ebionite version – how the Jewish followers of Jesus regarded him. There was no teaching about his deity; but there was a teaching of a Heavenly Messiah who incarnated in Jesus at his baptism. This doctrine was of Essene origin.

While the Hebrew Gospel sometimes gives a more reliable text, it is my view that in origin it is later than our canonical Gospels, and was in fact a response to them. The Jewish followers of Jesus had created a *Testimony* document and a *Teachings* document, which were among the sources of *Matthew* and *Luke*. But they had not needed a biographical type of work, such as was demanded by Gentile Christians, and certainly up to at least AD 60 they had the living witness both of the family of Jesus and of his immediate disciples. In particular, at the head of all believers in Jesus as Messiah, and to their entire satisfaction, there had been one who represented his status, his own brother Jacob.

In the Hebrew Gospel an account is given of the appearance of Jesus to his brother Jacob after the resurrection, which also Paul mentions (*I. Cor*. xv. 7). Jacob had sworn that he would neither eat nor drink until he had seen his brother risen from the dead.[6] Jacob was a very remarkable and significant individual, an ascetic who wore only linen garments like the Essenes. The records say that he was a regular visitor to the Temple at Jerusalem, where he spent long hours on his knees in prayer for his people. He was venerated by the Jewish populace, and accorded the honorific titles of 'the Just' and 'the People's Bastion',[7] and it is not going too far to say that his calming influence may well have helped to delay the Jewish revolt from Roman rule. Eventually, while Judea was temporarily without a Roman procurator, he and some others were seized by the hostile hierarchy on a trumped-up charge and executed in AD 62, which was a Sabbatical Year. The reigning high priest responsible was Ananus, another member of the Sadducean family notoriously opposed to Jesus and his followers. Many Jews protested to the new Roman governor, who promptly deposed Ananus from office.[8] It is significant that the Jewish historian Josephus, who was an admirer of the Essenes, put the fate of Jacob on record.

In various ancient sources in use by the Church Fathers the fame of Jacob is stressed. In the Clementine literature he is styled 'the supreme Supervisor, who rules Jerusalem, the holy Community of the Hebrews, and the communities everywhere excellently founded by the providence of God', and he is addressed as 'the Lord Jacob'.[9] In the *Gospel of Thomas*, recovered from Egypt, the disciples of Jesus ask him to whom they shall go when he has left them. Jesus replies, 'You will go to Jacob the Just, for whose sake heaven and earth were created.'

In the context of primitive Christianity, which was totally Jewish, there could be no doctrine of the deity of Jesus, and Jacob could no more have been the Brother of God than his mother was the Mother of God. In the text we have employed, when Jacob refers to his exalted brother it is the same terms Jesus himself used: he is styled the Son of *Man*. We shall be dealing with this theme in the next chapter.

In the Hebrew Gospel there was no Virgin Birth story. Jesus was the eldest child of Joseph and Mary, a fact preserved in the Synoptic Gospels. Jesus received Messiahship at the Jordan when he was baptised. The Hebrew Gospel makes much of this. The Spirit of God not only came upon Jesus: it entered into him. Spirit in Hebrew is feminine, and Jesus refers to the Holy Spirit as his mother in the Hebrew Gospel. Thus he was graced with 'the divinity that doth hedge a king'; and the circumstance makes much more sense of what followed his baptism, his acquisition of Messiahship, the account in his new capacity of his temptation in the wilderness.

For a true understanding of Jesus the testimony of the Fifth Gospel is indispensable.

NOTES AND REFERENCES

1. See Schonfield, *The Pentecost Revolution* (in USA: *The Jesus Party*).
2. See next chapter, p.113, Note 3.
3. *The Journal of Jewish Studies*, Vol. II, Nos. 2-3.
4. Challenging the views of a monk, Cyril of Jerusalem asked him where he obtained them, and was told 'from the Gospel written to the Hebrews.' 'Are there then five Gospels?' replied Cyril. See M. R. James, *The Apocryphal New Testament*, p. 8.

5. Schonfield, *According to the Hebrews* (Duckworth).
6. Jerome, *Of Illustrious Men*, 2 (see M. R. James: *The Apocryphal New Testament*, pp. 3-4).
7. Eusebius, *Ecclesiastical History*, II. xxiii.
8. Josephus, *Jewish Antiquities* XX. 200-203.
9. *Epistle of Clement to Jacob*.

15.

The Son of Man

The term which Jesus applied to himself for the greater part of his public activities was not the Christ (the Messiah). That, as I have pointed out,[1] would have assured his prompt arrest and execution by the Romans, since no one was allowed to claim to be a king, in this case King of the Jews, in any part of the Roman Empire without the authority of the emperor and senate. Jesus solved the problem by employing a pseudonym which would not give him away. He did not deny that he was the Messiah, but used a term for this personality created by the mysterious Brotherhood of the Essenes, unfamiliar to the Jewish populace[2] and having no political significance for the Romans. The question is, in describing himself as The Man (Son of Man) did this mean for Jesus what it meant for the Essenes? And did he embrace this doctrine as relating to himself? It would seem from the canonical Gospels and from Jewish Christian tradition that he did; and this throws a flood of light on the mentality and convictions of Jesus. It also helps to explain how Christianity came to go completely off the rails in its theology which concocted the Trinity.

The Essene impact on Primitive Christianity is demonstrable from the New Testament itself, and impressed itself on the earlier Christian historians. But once a Christian Creed was adopted, the Essene aspect was largely dropped or kept very much in the background. This is still the position for the vast majority of Christians, including the theologians. Historical inquiry in the late nineteenth century did resurrect many of the extra-canonical Jewish books, some of which were Essene works. And now, since the discovery of the Dead Sea Scrolls, we have been able to learn much more of the impact of Essene ideas and practices on Jesus and his followers. But still the consequences are resisted or ignored in Christian circles, for the very good reason that Christian theology would be overturned. One wonders for how long the truth will be suppressed.

In my book *The Essene Odyssey* I traced the origin and development of the Son of Man doctrine, and to this work I would direct the reader for more detailed information. The teaching of the Essenes in this respect derived from contact with the Iranian faith, as indeed did other elements in their imagination of the scheme of things. They accepted the concept of an eternal struggle between the forces of Light and Darkness, and they built their Messianic scheme on the idea of Mithra. Thus the Essenes were able to conceive of a Heavenly Man, in whose likeness the first man Adam was created (*Gen.* i. 26), and to identify that man with the Messiah (Christ) Above who in the redemptive process would incarnate in a human being, a Second Adam. Appropriately, therefore, *Luke* traces the descent of Jesus as Messiah from Adam 'who was the Son of God' (iii. 38).

The doctrine of the Heavenly Christ, the Archetypal Man, was peculiarly Essene. Partly it took its cue from *Daniel* vii. 13-14:

> I saw in the night visions, and, behold, one like a Son of Man [i.e. a human being, *Bar-Enosh*] came with the clouds of heaven, and came to the Ancient of Days, and they brought him near before him. And there was given him dominion, and glory, and a kingdom, that all people, nations, and languages, should serve him: his dominion is an everlasting dominion, which shall not pass away, and his kingdom that which shall not be destroyed.

Since this *Bar-Enosh* is described as king and world ruler he was conceived as the Messiah Above prepared by God before the creation for the ultimate government of our planet. But the conjunction was also made with the Earthly Messianic Hope, so that many believed that prior to the great climax of human history the heavenly anointed one (messiah) would incarnate in an earthly anointed one (prophet, priest and king). The Essenes thought of their True Teacher as such an incarnation, and later many followers of John the Baptist thought of him similarly, and so did many followers of Jesus believe the same of their master.

The most distinctive reference to the culmination of the human story in relationship to the Son of Man, the Heavenly Messiah, is found in the *Book of Enoch*, which the Early Christians believed to be divinely inspired (*I. Peter* iii. 19-20,[3] *Jude* 14-15). The section is well known to scholars.

The revelation of the Son of Man is given to the saintly Enoch:

And there I saw One who had a Head of Days [i.e. Daniel's Ancient of Days], and His head was white like wool. And with Him was another being whose countenance had the appearance of a man whose face was full of graciousness, like one of the holy angels. And I asked the angel who went with me and showed me all the hidden things, concerning that Son of Man, who he was and whence he was, and why he went with the Head of Days. And he answered and said unto me, 'This is the Son of Man who hath righteousness, and who reveals all the treasures of that which is hidden, because the Lord of Spirits hath chosen him... And this Son of Man whom thou hast seen... will put down the kings from their thrones and kingdoms because they do not extol and praise Him [i.e. the Lord of Spirits], nor thankfully acknowledge whence the kingdom was bestowed upon them...

And at that hour that the Son of Man was named in the presence of the Lord of Spirits and his name before the Head of Days. And before the sun and the signs were created, before the stars of heaven were made, his name was named before the Lord of Spirits. He will be a staff to the righteous on which they will support themselves and not fall, and he will be the light of the Gentiles and the hope of those who are troubled in heart. All who dwell on earth will fall down and bow the knee before him, and bless and laud and celebrate with song the Lord of Spirits. And for this cause has he been chosen and hidden before Him before the creation of the world...

And the Lord of Spirits seated him [the Son of Man] on the throne of his glory, and the spirit of righteousness was poured out upon him, and the word of his mouth slew all the sinners... And the righteous and elect will be saved on that day, and will never again from thenceforth see the faces of the sinners and unrighteous. And the Lord of Spirits will abide with them for ever, and with that Son of Man will they eat and drink and lie down and rise up for ever.[4]

The Essenes and Jewish mystics favoured what may be called the Law of Correspondences (as Above so Below). The earthly Adam was thus in the likeness of the heavenly Adam; there was a Jerusalem and a Temple above just as there was one below. But the heavenly had to descend and become united with the earthly, for the redemption of the world:

'A second Adam to the fight,
  and to the rescue came.'

The Son of Man above, the Archetypal Man, came to be regarded as the Heavenly Messiah who would incarnate in the Earthly Messiah. This was taught by the Essene wing of the Christians, known as the Ebionites (the Poor). They rejected the paganised doctrine of the Virgin Birth. Jesus was the son of Joseph and Mary, and became Christ (Messiah) at his baptism when the Christ Above, the Son of Man, had entered into him.

As it was handed down among the Ebionites, according to the fourth-century investigator Epiphanius:

Jesus was begotten of the seed of man, and was chosen; and so by the choice he was called Son of God from the Christ [Messiah] that entered into him from above in the likeness of a dove [i.e. at his baptism]. And they deny that he was begotten of God the Father, but say that he was created, as one of the archangels, yet greater, and that he is the lord of angels and of all things made by the Almighty. The Christ [Above], they say, is a Man-like figure, invisible to men in general.[5]

In the canonical Gospels, *Matthew*, *Mark* and *Luke*, there is a reflection of the incarnation of the Son of Man heavenly Christ, first of all in the circumstance that after the baptism of Jesus, when the conjunction was held to have taken place, he is led into the wilderness to be tempted of the Devil in his new capacity. Jesus now has powers that he did not have before. How is he to use them?

The revelation of this incarnation is not given to the Apostles until shortly before Jesus is to manifest himself publicly as Messiah, and then only to his three intimates Peter, James and John. There is set down the account of the Transfiguration on the Mount. The Son of Man in Jesus is made manifest by his face shining as the sun, and his raiment becoming white as the light. Moses and Elijah appear and speak with him. And further, a voice out of the clouds proclaims what Jesus himself heard when the heavenly Christ had entered him at his baptism (*Matthew* xvii, *Mark* ix, *Luke* ix).

It is to be noted that the Transfiguration story is immediately preceded by the words of Jesus about the Son of Man. 'The Son of Man shall come in the glory of his Father with his angels; and then he shall reward every man according to his works. Truly I say unto you, there are some standing here who will not taste of death till they see the Son of Man coming in his kingdom.' This is in line with the coming of the Son of Man in *Enoch*, and indeed in the Son of Man passages in the New Testament. We have to represent these passages, and consider how far they reflect the convictions of Jesus himself, and how far they are the interpretations of the early Jewish Christians under strong Essene influence.

I have rightly stressed the Essene influence on Christian beginnings, which the recovery of the Dead Sea Scrolls has put beyond a shadow of doubt. We can now clearly see the Essenism in the New Covenant (Testament), the significance of Pentecost, the organisation of the Early Church, the distribution of goods, the descriptions and references such as 'the Poor' and 'the Way', the manner of interpreting the Old Testament as Messianically predictive of circumstances and events, and so on. The Son of Man concept was at the heart of this Essenism.

Consequently we ought to allow that this Essenism was to an extent reflected backwards in the presentation of Jesus in the Gospels, as in the Transfiguration story, and in that of his ultimate bodily Ascension. Certain sayings attributed to Jesus could also have resulted, especially in the Fourth Gospel. But making allowance for all this it seems impossible to set aside completely that Jesus did present himself as the Son of Man of the Jewish mystics. And if he did so we must face up to the implications in considering his mentality. Here, then, are a few of the statements Jesus makes in the Gospels:

> Whosoever therefore shall be ashamed of me and of my words in this adulterous and sinful generation, of him also shall the Son of Man be ashamed, when he cometh in the glory of his Father with the holy angels. (*Mark* viii. 38)

> In those days, after that tribulation, the sun shall be darkened, and the moon shall not give her light... And then shall they see the Son of Man coming in the clouds with great power and glory. And then shall he send his angels, and shall gather together his elect from the four winds, from the uttermost part of the earth to the uttermost part of heaven. (*Mark* xiii. 24-27)

> Again the High Priest asked him, and said unto him, Art thou the Messiah [Christ]...? And Jesus said, I am; and ye shall see

110

the Son of Man sitting on the right hand of Power, and coming in the clouds of heaven. (*Mark* xiv. 61-62)

The Son of Man shall send forth his angels, and they shall gather out of his kingdom all things that offend, and them which do iniquity, and shall cast them into a furnace of fire. (*Matthew* xiii. 41-42)

The Son of Man shall come in the glory of his Father with his angels; and then shall he reward every man according to his works. Verily I say unto you, There be some standing here, which shall not taste of death, till they see the Son of Man coming in his kingdom. (*Matthew* xvi. 27-28)

And Jesus said unto them [i.e. the Twelve], Verily I say unto you, that ye which have followed me, in the regeneration when the Son of Man shall sit on the throne of his glory, ye also shall sit upon twelve thrones, judging the twelve tribes of Israel. (*Matthew* xix. 28)

And then shall appear the sign of the Son of Man in heaven... (*Matthew* xxiv. 30 *et seq.*)

There are comparable passages in *Luke*, which we need not cite, and we shall be dealing with *John* in the next chapter. One thing we must note from the references quoted, as regards their authenticity, is allusion to circumstances which have a bearing on dates. Since the Twelve are to judge the twelve tribes of Israel the betrayal by Judas would not seem at the time to have been anticipated. The return to the world of the Son of Man, when he is to take his throne, is to take place not only during the lifetime of some listening to Jesus, but the contemporary High Priest and members of the Sanhedrin will also be alive and witness the event. When history contradicted all of these things one would expect an attempt to delete or modify them on the part of the Gospel writers. That they did not, conveys faithfulness to sources regarded as too authoritative to tamper with.

Additionally, it is of consequence that in the Synoptic Gospels the expression Son of God is never used by Jesus in relation to himself. On the very rare occasions where it occurs it is almost entirely hostile persons and spirits who employ it.

That the Son of Man doctrine of the Essenes in relation to Jesus was in evidence from the very beginning of the Christian community is confirmed by the fact that it was familiar to the Apostle Paul. Unfortunately, because the Church adopted the Trinitarian formula and held Jesus to be Divine, it has not correctly understood Paul's doctrine and misrepresented it in the translation of his words from the Greek. I give here two passages as they should be interpreted. First from *Colossians*:

[For Paul, the Messiah (Christ) as Archetypal Man is]
the image of the Unseen God [*Gen.* i. 26-27], the Firstborn of Creation, that everything in heaven and earth might be founded on him, seen and unseen alike, whether angelic Thrones or Lordships or Rulers or Authorities. Everything was created through him and for him. He is the antecedent of everything, and on him [i.e. as the Archetype] everything was framed. So also is he the head of the Body, the Community [Church], that is to say, the fount and origin of it, the firstborn from the dead, that in every connection he might take precedence. For it pleased God that by him the whole [i.e. of Creation] should be governed (*Col.* i. 15-19).

The other passage is in *Philippians*. Paul writes:

Let your disposition be that of the Messiah Jesus, who though he had godlike form [i.e. as Archetype] did not [like the earthly Adam] regard it as a prize to be equal to God [*Gen.* iii. 5-6], but divested himself [i.e. put off the garment of light], taking the form of a servant. Appearing in human likeness, and disclosed in physical appearance as a man, he abased himself, and became subject to death, death by the cross. That is why God has so exalted him, that at the name of Jesus every knee, heavenly, earthly and infernal, should bend, and every tongue acclaim Jesus Christ as lord, to the glory of God the Father. (*Phil.* ii. 5-11)

Paul has no suspicion of the fourth-century conception that the Son was 'not made, nor created, but begotten'. The Son of Man was created as the visible expression of God, but in no sense God Himself, whom no eye can see, and who has neither form nor substance. Nowhere does Paul call Jesus God. 'There is One God, and one mediator between God and men, *the man* Christ Jesus' (*I. Tim.* ii. 5).

Notes and References

1. See above, Chapter 12.
2. The Son of Man concept of the Jewish mystics was unfamiliar to the Jewish populace (*John* xii. 34) and not identified with the Messiah.
3. As Moffatt noted, by a scribal error the name Enoch was dropped out of *I. Peter* iii. 19, by a dittograph of the Greek for 'by which'. The text should read: 'By which Enoch also went and preached unto the spirits in prison...' The circumstances are related in the *Book of Enoch*.
4. See the *Book of Enoch*, the Similitudes, xlvi. 1-5, xlviii. 2-10, lxii. 2-14 (edited and translated by R. H. Charles).
5. Epiphanius, *Panarion* xxx. 21. (See also M. R. James: *The Apocryphal New Testament*, Clarendon Press, Oxford, 1969, p. 10).

16.

The Johannine Puzzle

There are several documents in the New Testament ascribed to someone called John. There is the Fourth Gospel, the three Epistles in which the author simply refers to himself as the Elder, and the *Revelation* stated to have been given by an angel to John the servant of Jesus. It is commonly held that all of these documents were the work of one man, called in the Gospel 'the Dear Disciple.' And it is very widely supposed that this individual was one of the Twelve, the fisherman John the son of Zebedee. Nothing could be further from the truth.

Imagination simply will not do. We have to seek for evidence, both in the language and statements of the books themselves and in what has been preserved in early Christian tradition. This undertaking is essential because we need to know how far the words put into the mouth of Jesus in the Fourth Gospel are reliable, since he speaks so differently to the Jesus of the Synoptic Gospels. And not only does he speak differently; what is related about him is substantially an alternative and occasionally a contradictory story.

In the Fourth Gospel the Son of Man aspect is even more distinctively Essene and readily asserted by Jesus in respect of his heavenly derivation:

> No man hath ascended up to heaven, but he that came down from heaven, even the Son of Man which is in heaven [*John* iii. 13].
> I came down from heaven, not to do mine own will, but the will of Him that sent me [vi. 38]. What and if ye shall see the Son of Man ascend up where he was before? [vi. 62]

Paul thought of the Son of Man in his incarnation as divesting himself of his heavenly nature and exhibiting himself as a servant. Not so the Fourth Gospel. There, in a most unpleasant manner, Jesus glorifies himself publicly and privately, and makes no attempt to conceal his superhumanity. And there is added in places not only an insolence and boastfulness, but some very un-Jewish and even anti-Jewish traits. There is in evidence a very substantial departure from the human historical Jesus seeking his people's deliverance and commitment to the responsibilities of being 'a light to the Gentiles.' A superhuman Jesus is represented who is the kind of personality which seems fitting to the author of the three Epistles. If one reads them carefully one finds that very largely in the Gospel Jesus speaks in the manner of the writer of the Epistles.

But before we can come to grips with the contents and structure of the Gospel it is essential to consider what tradition has to tell us about the Dear Disciple and the creation of the Fourth Gospel. From the Gospel itself we learn that the Dear Disciple was initially a disciple of John the Baptist, a Messianist with Essene leanings. He could well have been of priestly stock, since he was personally known to the High Priest and a familiar figure at his palace; and also when it was reported that the tomb to which Jesus had been taken was open the Dear Disciple will not enter it until he knows there is no body there and therefore he will not incur ritual defilement. The Dear Disciple had a house in Jerusalem, which became the home of the mother of Jesus. There is a very strong probability that this was the house in which the Last Supper was held, whose owner must have been highly trusted by Jesus, and which was very roomy. It is no less probable, on the evidence, that there the phenomenon of Pentecost took place. It was fitting that at the Last Supper, as disclosed in the Fourth Gospel, the Dear Disciple as Master of the House should recline on the breast of Jesus who was the guest of honour. Jesus himself reclined on the breast of his principal disciple Peter. We note in the Gospel that Peter is somewhat jealous of the Dear Disciple, but also depends on him in the alien and sophisticated atmosphere of Jerusalem.

It is communicated at the end of the Gospel that the Dear Disciple would live to a great age, so that the belief arose that he would not die before the return of Jesus to the world. And what would be quite extraordinary if the Dear Disciple had been one of the Twelve, the Gospel provides a certification by some authorities of the *bona fides* of the author: 'This is the disciple which testifieth of these things, and wrote these things: and *we know* that his testimony is true' (*John* xxi. 24). If the disciple was John the son of Zebedee with whom all Christians were familiar why not say so? And what was a humble fisherman doing with a large house in Jerusalem? That John the son of Zebedee and the owner of the house were two different persons is plainly stated by *Luke*, for he says that this John with Peter were the two disciples whom Jesus sent to the master of the house. (*Luke* xxii. 8-12)

But what then of the author of the *Revelation*, who is also called John? This man is a person of some authority, for he writes letters of exhortation to seven Christian communities in Roman Asia, to Ephesus, Smyrna, Pergamos, Thyatira, Sardis, Philadelphia and Laodicea. He does not say he is John son of Zebedee the Apostle of Jesus. He describes himself simply as 'your brother, and companion in tribulation, and in the kingdom and patience of Jesus Christ' (*Rev.* i. 9). He states that on account of his convictions he had been on Patmos, a small island off the coast, where he had visions.

The first vision he had was not of the human Jesus but of the heavenly Son of Man who had, according to the Jewish Christians, incarnated in Jesus. He heard a long strident voice like the sound of a trumpet, and when he turned to see the speaker he saw someone 'who appeared as the Son of Man. He wore a long robe with a golden girdle at the chest. His head and his hairs were white like wool, as white as snow; and his eyes were as flames of fire, and his feet like burnished bronze' (*Rev.* i. 13-15). The apparition claims to be the First and the Last, that is, the Archetypal Man in heaven and the Second Adam in his incarnation in Jesus. In the letter to the Laodician Community he is 'the beginning of God's creation' (iii. 14, and see *Col.* i. 15 and *Gen.* i. 26-27). But, curiously, the description of the Son of Man is that which in *Daniel* vii. 9 is assigned to the Ancient of Days. The Son of Man is described in *Daniel* x. 5-6 in exalted but other terms. No Jewish writer would have made such an error. So here we have one of a number of indications that in the Johannine literature we have to do with more than one John, none of them being the son of Zebedee. Tradition helps us here, as we shall now illustrate, but we have also to study very closely in the Greek – which the general reader cannot do – the style, ideas and attitudes reflected in the text.[1]

What we note immediately in tradition is the association of the John personalities with Asia Minor. We would suspect this from the fact that the author of the *Revelation* was exiled to Patmos off the coast of that region, and subsequently communicated with seven

Christian communities there. Also there is a very strong probability that the hymn to Christ as the light, with which the Gospel commences, is in fact the very same antiphonal hymn referred to by the younger Pliny at the beginning of the second century when he was the governor of Bithynia in Asia Minor. In his famed letter to Trajan about the Christians he states how by torturing Christians he had learnt that they were accustomed to sing an antiphonal hymn to Christ just before dawn. In my translation of *John*'s Gospel I have set out the hymn in its real character.[2] And as this is a matter of some consequence as well as general interest, I may give it here. The response is in italics.

In the beginning was the Word.
> *And the Word was with God.*

So the Word was divine.
> *He was in the beginning with God.*

By him everything had being.
> *And without him nothing had being.*

What had being by him was Life.
> *And Life was the Light of men.*

And the Light shines in the Darkness.
> *And the Darkness could not suppress it.*

This was the true Light.
> *It illumines all who enter the world.*

He was in the world, [and the world had being by him]
> *But the world did not recognise him.*

He came to his own domains.
> *And his own did not receive him.*

The Word took bodily form and dwelt with us.
> *And we beheld his glory.*

Glory as of the Father's Only-begotten.
> *Full of loving-kindness and truth.*

For of his bounty have we all received.
> *Yes, mercy added to mercy.*

For the Law was given by Moses.
> Loving-kindness and truth came by Jesus Christ.

The Church Father Eusebius believed the Essenes to be Primitive Christians, and in his *Ecclesiastical History* he has also something to tell us about the John matters. He refers to the statements of an Asian Christian, Papias of Hierapolis, who in a famous work *Exe-*

gesis of the Dominical Oracles, had spoken of John the Elder as distinct from John the Beloved Disciple. Papias had flourished in the first half of the second century AD. Distinguishing the two Johns, Eusebius refers to information that at Ephesus there were two tombs, both of them described as John's.[3] At another place in his *History* he speaks of the John who was the Beloved Disciple as a priest, indeed as having acted as Jewish High Priest, and who died in Asia Minor, citing a letter from the bishop Polycrates to Victor bishop of Rome.[4]

In my book *Those Incredible Christians*, published by Hutchinson, I went into the whole subject in the chapter 'The Man Called John', being greatly aided by what my friend Robert Eisler had written in his valuable work *The Enigma of the Fourth Gospel* (Methuen). The traditions indicate that John the Beloved Disciple having returned from exile in Patmos lived to a great age. Complying with Christian desire he finally dictated his reminiscences. This material came into the hands of a strong-minded and opinionated Elder of non-Jewish origin, who took over the manuscript and used part of it interspersed with his own doctrine. He also edited the *Revelation* and introduced among other passages the Letters to the Seven Churches. The long speeches of Jesus in the Gospel and the long comments are the work of the Elder. These, unfortunately, are among the elements that Christians rely on so much, and which have no authenticity as reflecting the views of Jesus himself. To a very appreciable extent we can separate the wheat from the chaff, and it is essential to do so if we are genuinely seeking to discover the real Jesus. So supreme is the Johannine material in the teaching of the Church of today that it takes great courage, knowledge and understanding, for a Christian to apprehend and acknowledge that much that is put into the mouth of Jesus, or appears to be ascribed to him, is the invention of the non-Jewish Elder, who had never companied with Jesus.

How non-Jews in the first century AD could express belief in themselves as God incarnate is well illustrated by the Roman emperors Gaius Caligula, Nero and Domitian. The first of these megalomaniacs, shortly after the time of Jesus, sought to have his statue set up for worship in the Temple at Jerusalem, and nearly went to war with the Jews when they refused to permit this. About this man I quote the Roman historian Suetonius:

> Having extended part of the Palatium as far as the Forum, and the temple of Castor and Pollux being converted into a kind of vestibule to his house, he often stationed himself between the

twin brothers, and so presented himself to be worshipped by all
votaries; some of whom saluted him by the name *Jupiter
Latiaris*. He also instituted a temple and priests, with choice
victims, in honour of his own divinity. In his temple stood a
statue of gold, the exact image of himself, which was daily
dressed in garments corresponding with those he wore himself...
On nights when the moon was full, he was in the constant habit
of inviting her to his embraces and his bed. In the day-time he
talked in private to Jupiter Capitolinus.[5]

Of course Gaius was mad, but Domitian emphasised his deity
more in arrogance and to bolster his authority. Of him Suetonius says
that:

When he dictated the form of a letter to be used by his procu-
rators, he began it thus: 'Our Lord and God commands so and
so'; whence it became a rule that no one should style him otherwise either in writing or speaking.[6]

How many have noticed that in the Fourth Gospel (*John* xx. 28)
the Apostle Thomas is made to address Jesus in the very same form,
'My Lord and my God'? And how many have recognised that the
Elder's Jesus, in the Fourth Gospel, is nearly as much of an arrogant
egomaniac as these Caesars? Let us hear him speak as the Elder
makes him. It may seem harsh to do this; but in all honesty it is
essential as far as we can to ascertain how much has been preserved
of the real Jesus, and how much is misrepresentation. We shall quote
only words stated to have been used by Jesus.[7]

Jesus said to them, 'I tell you for a positive fact, if you do not
eat the flesh of the Son of Man and drink his blood you will
not have life in yourselves. Whoever chews my flesh and drinks
my blood will have eternal life, and I must raise him up on the
Last Day; for my flesh is true food and my blood is true drink.
Whoever chews my flesh and drinks my blood continues in me,
and I in him. Just as the Living Father has sent me, and I live
through the Father, so he who chews me will likewise live
through me.' (*John* vi. 53-57)

The Pharisees said to him, 'You are testifying on your own
behalf. Your testimony is not valid.' Jesus replied, 'Though I
testify on my own behalf my testimony is valid, for I know
where I came from and where I am going... But if I were to

judge, my judgement would be valid because I am not alone. There is myself and Him who has sent me. And in your Law it is stated that the testimony of two persons is valid. There is myself who am testifying on my own behalf, and there is the Father who has sent me who testifies on my behalf.' (*John* viii. 13-18)

Jesus said to them [i.e. the Jews], 'If God were your Father you would love me, for I emanated and came from God. I did not come of my own accord; He sent me. How is it you do not recognise my voice? It is because you cannot heed my message. You have the Devil for a father, and would carry out your father's behests. He was a manslayer from the very first, and could never abide the truth; for truth is alien to him. When he utters a lie he speaks his own language; for he is a liar and the father of lies. But because I speak the truth you do not believe me. Whoever belongs to God heeds the words of God. The very fact that you do not heed me proves that you do not belong to God.' (*John* viii. 42-47)

So Jesus spoke again [i.e. to the Jews], 'I tell you for a positive fact, I am the door for the sheep. All those who came before me are thieves and robbers; but the sheep have not listened to them. I am the door. Whoever enters by me will be safe, and will come in and go out, and find pasture. The thief only comes to steal and kill and destroy. I have come that they may have life and ever more life. I tell you for a positive fact, whoever does not use the door to the sheep-pen, but gets in another way, is a thief and a robber.' (*John* x. 7-10)

[The Jews say] 'If you are the Messiah, tell us plainly.' Jesus replied, 'I have told you, and you do not believe because you do not belong to my sheep. My sheep listen to my voice, and I know them, and they follow me. And I will give them Eternal Life, and they will never perish, and no one shall wrest them from my hand. My Father who has given me everything is stronger, and no one can wrest anything from my Father's hand. I and the father are one...' (*John* x. 24-30)

'Is it not stated in your Law, I said, you are gods [*Ps.* lxxxii. 6]? If He called them gods to whom God's message came, and there is no evading the Scripture, how can you say to him whom the Father consecrated and sent into the world, you blaspheme, because I said I am God's Son? If I do not perform my Father's miracles, do not believe me, believe the miracles, that you may realise and recognise that the Father is in me and I am in the Father. (*John* x. 34-38)

Jesus then cried, 'Whoever believes in me, does not believe in me, but in Him who has sent me. And he who sees me, sees Him who has sent me.' (*John* xii. 44-45)

Jesus said to him [i.e. Thomas], 'I myself am Way and Truth and Life. No one reaches the Father except by me. If you knew me, you would also perceive my Father. From now on you do know Him, and have seen Him.' Philip said to him, 'Show us the Father, Master, and we shall be content.' Jesus replied, 'Have I been with you all so long, yet you have not recognised me Philip? He who has seen me has seen the Father. Why then do you say, Show us the Father? Do you not believe that I am in the Father, and that the Father is in me?' (*John* xiv. 6-10)

'If they have persecuted me, they will also persecute you. If they have not heeded my message, neither will they heed yours... If I had not come and spoken to them no sin would have been theirs, but now they have no excuse for their sin. He who hates me hates the Father also.' (*John* xv. 20-23)

'I have spoken to you enigmatically thus far. The time will come when I shall no longer speak to you enigmatically, but will inform you about the Father plainly. When that time comes you will ask in my name, and I will not say to you, I will ask the Father on your behalf. The Father Himself will love you, because you have loved me and believed that I came from the Father and entered the world. Now I am leaving the world again and going to the Father.' (*John* xvi. 25-28)

[Jesus said] 'Father, the time has come. Glorify Thy Son, that Thy Son may glorify Thee, just as Thou gavest Him authority over all flesh, so that to all whom Thou hast given him he should grant Eternal Life.' (*John* xvii. 1-2)

Here we have a bombastic pagan Jesus, who speaks as no Jew possibly could, the creation of a man who tries to do his best to imagine how a God-man might express himself in a Jewish context. If John the Elder had been writing today he might well have presented Jesus in science-fiction form, as an alien from another planet on a mission to our Earth. The visitor would find it extremely difficult to explain where he has come from and what he has come for, and to acclimatise himself to our environment. He also might well be extremely irritated by our stupidity and unresponsiveness, and hit back with threats and denunciations. As it is we have a man who is a caricature of deity and pathologically pretentious in his humanity.

It could be inferred that what caused John the Elder to latch on to the legacy of John the Priest, the Beloved Disciple, was precisely because that aged disciple had been so strongly devoted to the Essene Son of Man doctrine. In presenting Jesus in this guise he went very much further than the authors of the other canonical Gospels, and thus gave the Greek Elder his chance to interpret Jesus in his own Gentile fashion[8] which had the semblance of affinity with the proto-type.

Because of the composite character of this Gospel, its inter-polations, comments and disarray of part of the text, it is not easy to identify all the elements, and certain conclusions have therefore to be tentative. It is also very important to appreciate that nearly all the references to the Jews are not references to Jews in the religious sense, but in the geographical sense, the inhabitants of Judea as compared with those of Galilee. In the time of Jesus the country was divided into three areas, Galilee, Samaria and Judea. Religiously the Galileans were also Jews, but these northerners were largely of different stock than the southerners and strongly independent, using their own dialect. While Jesus lived in Galilee, and his immediate disciples were Galileans, he himself was a Jew both by religion and descent, belonging to the royal tribe of Judah. It would be preferable, therefore, in many of the references to 'the Jews' to substitute 'Judeans'. The Greek has the same word *Ioudaioi* in both connections. Failure to point out the circumstances has been responsible for much Christian anti-Jewish feeling.

NOTES AND REFERENCES

1. The reader is referred to my translation of the New Testament from the Greek, *The Original New Testament*, and to my book *Those Incredible Christians*.

2. See *The Original New Testament*, and the *Letter of Pliny to Trajan* (Loeb Classical Library).
3. Eusebius, *Eccl. Hist.* Bk. III. xxxix.
4. Ibid. Bk. V. xxiv.
5. Suetonius, *Lives of the Caesars*, Gaius (Caligula), ch. xxii.
6. Ibid. Domitian, ch. xiii.
7. For clarity, I have employed here my own direct rendering of the Greek.
8. No Jew would dream of speaking as the Elder makes Jesus speak, and only a non-Jew would make Jesus refer to '*your* Law', since it was the Law which God gave to Moses, and for a divine Jesus *his* Law. The Fourth Gospel is unique in referring to Greeks who wish to meet Jesus (*John* xii. 21).

17.

Limitations

There are traits of kindness and affection in the Jesus of the Fourth Gospel, but they are outweighed by arrogance and hostility towards those who thwart or oppose him. The Jesus of the other Gospels is a much more natural person, Jewish in his faith and therefore with no pretensions to deity. But he does believe he is the Messiah, the ultimate king of Israel of David's line, and that he has been invested with the attributes of the heavenly Archetypal Man, the Messiah Above of the Jewish mystics.

Let us now look frankly at how Jesus is depicted in the Synoptics, which to an appreciable extent do reflect personal memories of him. He is first of all a man in humble circumstances, the eldest member of a large family resident in a small town in Galilee. His father, who would seem to have died when he was in his teens, had been an artisan; and with so many mouths to feed – four younger brothers and at least two sisters – he would have known very early in life what it was like to be poor and sometimes hungry. In *Luke*'s version of the famous Sermon (vi. 20-38) the first to receive consolation in the coming Kingdom of God on Earth are the poor, the hungry and the bereaved. The word 'blessed' in the Greek does not quite reflect the Hebrew word Jesus would have used, *ashrei*, 'happy are you'.

But Jesus was no country bumpkin. His pious father was an intelligent man, proud of his royal descent, and cherishing the conviction that his eldest was destined to be the deliverer of Israel. He could well have nourished this conviction in the boy Jesus, instructing him in the Scriptures and especially in the Psalms of David. *Luke*'s story of Jesus in the Temple, listening to the learned teachers and eagerly asking them questions, is meant to convey that he was a bright child, and already busy with imagination of his Messianic destiny. Nothing is related of Jesus's experiences in early manhood;

124

but we can deduce from the Gospels that these years were ones of preparation in which he sought to enquire what was the mission and destiny of the Messiah. In this pursuit he would certainly have wished to encounter the Essenes, since they were the principal architects of the Messianic and skilled in the interpretation of the prophecies in terms of their fulfilment and the Signs of the Times. Josephus records how Herod the Great as a boy had been told by the Essene Menahem that he would be a king when he had no such prospect and was not even of royal blood.[1] From the Essenes and some of their books which were in circulation Jesus would have gained a certain apprehension of their Son of Man teaching. Another source would have been the convictions of the Pharisees. What further makes it seem probable that Jesus resorted especially to the Essenes was his evident gifts as a healer and exorcist, gifts for which they were famed.

Another thing the Synoptic Gospels convey is that Jesus was very sensitive and poetic. He felt it when a woman touched him, even though he was being jostled by a crowd.[2] Poetry, notably with its Hebraic parallelism, enters into his utterances and parables.[3] He was extremely observant, as is evident from the stories he told largely drawn from life and covering aspects relating to farming and fishing, commerce and social circumstances. But evidently he was not too robust, and tired easily. His languages were Hebrew and Aramaic, and he would be familiar with the Galilean dialect. He would also know some Greek and a smattering of Latin.

The Galileans were highly superstitious, and their handling of Judaism was rather flexible. But they broadly adhered to the Jewish faith and its observances, keeping the sabbaths and festivals and making the pilgrimages to the Temple at Jerusalem. The Pharisees, who were evangelical democrats, had largely created the synagogues in Galilee as places of worship and instruction. But they had difficulty in inducing the Galileans to stick to the rules in the dogmatic forms and interpretations the Pharisees favoured. Where the Galileans stood out was in their sturdy nationalism and independent spirit. Here they might be said to be even more Jewish than the Judeans, ever ready to fight alien rulers and authorities.

In some respects Jesus was typically Galilean. He approved the devotion of the Pharisees to the Laws of Moses, but not their parading of their piety, which tended towards hypocrisy, their Bible punching and preaching of hell-fire and damnation while failing to reflect the spirit of the teaching, its sensitivity and humanity.[4]

Like the Pharisees the unaristocratic Jesus had little respect for the Sadducees, though he encountered them but rarely in the north. They were known not to interpret the Bible prophetically and messianically, and their teaching could thus allow them to come to terms with the alien Occupying Power, provided it did not threaten their religion, and with the priestly aristocracy and their privileges. Substantially the Sadducees were the party of Jewish government, in which the chief priests had long played a leading part. Thus they could be described as high churchmen, caught up in an environment of ceremonial and institution. Inevitably their religion had a patronising and commercial aspect, and their ritualism and authority inclined them to despise the Jewish masses, whose patriotism they also had reason to fear. Jesus was very much a Galilean in his attitude to the chief priests and their minions.

Reading the histories of Josephus alongside the Gospels and the *Acts of the Apostles* we can appreciate much more realistically and truthfully the nature of the animus between the chief priests with their supporters and the strongly nationalistic popular party of combined Christians and Pharisees. The situation was steadily to deteriorate, with those who represented the Messianic finally overthrowing the chief priests and going to war with the Romans. The climax of the life of Jesus was already a portent of what was to come, with its stress on the conflict between the Jewish people and those who were ruling them. In finally riding into Jerusalem as king of the Jews Jesus made it very clear whose side he was on. Nothing could be more revealing of the Jewish nationalism of Jesus.[5] At the climax of his career he was the hero and darling of his people.

When examined carefully, and without religious bias and pious sentiment, the Synoptic Gospels reveal Jesus throughout his public life as a skilled tactician with a very positive programme. He did not go about preaching and healing aimlessly. His choice of the Twelve, reflecting the number of the tribes of Israel, and his instructions to them, well illustrates his purposefulness; so, towards the end, does his concentration on Jerusalem at the Passover as the moment of his public disclosure of his Messiahship. He was no milk and water Messiah, or for that matter a demonstrator of the character of Deity. He believed he had been chosen by God as king of Israel, to bring his people back to the fulfilment of their world mission, and he meant to fulfil his own rôle to the uttermost. Jesus was not a man of the world or a public school type. He had an artisan's upbringing in a provincial environment. He was very observant of individuals, and had something of a lower class aptitude for argument and denunciation, as well as a capacity for plotting and devising stratagems. In certain respects he was narrowly parochial. I went into these aspects of his nature in some detail in my book *The Passover Plot*.

Throughout his public life Jesus never crossed the borders of the Land of Israel, or visited any heathen home. In only one or two cases did he heal Gentiles, when it was evident that there was acknowledgement of the God of Israel (*Matt.* xv. 22-28; *Luke* vii. 1-8). In *Matthew*'s version of the healing of the centurion's servant, in the passage I have cited from *Luke* – the centurion who loves the Jews and has built them a synagogue – there is an added saying of Jesus (*Matt.* viii. 11). Here the Kingdom of God is to be set up in the Land of Israel. In those days many Gentiles 'shall come from the East and the West [i.e. in the Messianic Age], and recline with Abraham, Isaac and Jacob [the Hebrew Patriarchs] in the Kingdom of Heaven.' The pious Gentiles will come to the Holy Land, as in the vision of the Hebrew prophets. There is no indication of a task of world evangelisation for the Apostles such as was tacked on to the end of the Synoptic Gospels.

Despite his naiveté and limitations, and perhaps because of them, Jesus could get to the root of things to an extent that might well have not been practicable for a more sophisticated person. From experience and acute observation Jesus had a considerable understanding of human nature: he was shrewd but also very sentimental and sympathetic. Of the world at large he did not know a great deal. His judgements and decisions were not always sound on the evidence of the Synoptics. We may give here a few illustrations.

Jesus chose as his Messianic emissaries twelve humble local people out of all Israel, and told them that when he came to the throne they would sit on twelve thrones judging the twelve tribes (*Matt.* xix. 27-29). He does not seem to have any idea then that one of them would betray him. He also promised that all who had abandoned family or lands for his sake would receive a hundredfold in his kingdom. The cities that would not receive the message of the Twelve would be punished in the Day of Judgement worse than Sodom and Gomorrha (*Matt.* x. 14-15). Similarly, Jesus denounced the small townships in Galilee, such as Chorazin, Bethsaida and Capernaum, for failing to repent at his message. Their fate in the Day of Judgement would be worse than that of Tyre and Sidon,

Sodom [and Gomorrha] (*Matt.* xi. 20-24). It is evident that he was becoming very bitter at his lack of success in his Galilean local environment, which constituted the area in which he was chiefly active. The world abroad did not come within the framework of his knowledge and experience. Sheba, whose queen had visited Solomon to learn of his wisdom, was not a great distance from the Holy Land, but for Jesus that country was 'the uttermost parts of the earth' (*Matt.* xii. 42)

Jesus comes before us as very much a man of his time and country, and none the worse for that. His faith and dedication were most admirable, and there is much we can learn from him, especially in Messianic matters. But he was no exemplification either of human perfection or of divine omniscience, for which we must be truly thankful.

NOTES AND REFERENCES

1. Josephus, *Jewish Antiquities*, Bk. XV, 373-378.
2. *Mark* v. 25-34.
3. *Matt.* vi. 1; *Luke* vi. 37; and cf. *Zechariah* ix. 9.
4. *Matt.* xxiii. 23.
5. *Matt.* xxi. 1-9.

18.

Derivations

The view of Jesus I have represented in the previous chapters was derived from an objective reading of the Gospels, particularly the first three. With the Fourth Gospel a very different Jesus was portrayed. In dealing with that Gospel I gave my reasons for concluding that a great part of what is said by Jesus and about Jesus is the creation of an individual who wished to present a Christ of his own contriving, an alien to his people and environment. Among matters we have to consider now is whether the Jesus of the other Gospels is also to an extent fictitious.

John the Elder was not the only New Testament writer who had not known Jesus personally to give his own conception of him and his function. The author of the *Epistle to the Hebrews*, believed by many to be Apollos, did so, basing his ideas very largely on the mystical teaching of Philo of Alexandria. Paul too had never met the physical Jesus. He had learned a few things about his life and teaching, but had created his own interpretation of his character and significance. He did not want to know the human Jesus, only the spiritual one. 'Though we have known Christ after the flesh, yet now henceforth know we him no more... old things are passed away' (*II. Cor.* v. 16-17). In all Paul's letters only one saying of Jesus is quoted, one that is not in the Gospels and reveals nothing of his personality. As a religious teacher, who was also a Roman citizen, Paul inevitably played down as much as he could the Jewishness and political aspect of Jesus as a Messiah. He referred to him as Jesus Christ, not as Jesus *the* Christ. Paul was inevitably greatly disturbed when apostles from Jerusalem revealed to his converts a very different Jesus, a Messiah who was a practising Jew.

Paul emphasised the superiority of his Gospel. 'I neither received it of man, neither was I taught it, but by the revelation of Jesus

Christ' (*Gal*. i. 12). He cursed those who were removing his converts to 'another Gospel, which is not another' (*Gal*. i. 6-7) and 'preaching another Jesus, whom we have not preached' (*II. Cor.* xi. 4). But the Jesus and the Gospel that was anathema to Paul was the Jesus of those who had companied with him, the teaching of his native followers, now headed by his own brother Jacob (James) and by Peter.

In the century following the Jewish war with the Romans (AD 66-70) the new religion of Christianity took shape, with predominantly non-Jewish adherents, and this state of affairs was to continue down to the present day. A great number of the Jewish followers of Jesus, including many who had seen and heard him, perished or were scattered as a consequence of the war, though some, including members of his family, managed to escape to the north-east. Here they were largely isolated from Christians in other lands, and could not exert much influence on Christian developments. The war had had another effect. The defeat of the Jews intensified the considerable amount of antisemitism in the Mediterranean area, and inevitably the churches in Greece, Egypt and Asia Minor were infected by it. Here Paul's attitude was influential, and the first collection of Christian documents was the Pauline Epistles.

In works like the *Acts of the Apostles* and the *Second Epistle of Peter* it was played down that the views of Peter, who was strongly opposed to Paul, having known Jesus so well, should take precedence. In the bogus second letter, 'Peter' refers to certain things in Paul's letters 'by no means easy to understand, which the unskilled and unstable twist to their own ruination as they do the rest of the Scriptures' (*II. Peter* iii. 16). The denomination of Paul's letters as Scripture quite gives the game away. Those who represented the historical Jesus thus came to be denounced as the Judaisers, and this attitude was to persist and intensify down the centuries. When the great Greek codices of the Bible were written in the fourth century the animus against the Jews was particularly severe.

The patron of the new Christian orthodoxy, the Emperor Constantine, had declared: 'We desire to have nothing in common with this so hated people, for the Redeemer has marked out another path for us. To this we will keep, and be free from disgraceful association with this people.' The Jewish convert to Christianity had publicly in church to 'renounce absolutely everything Jewish, every law, rite and custom.'[1] The convictions of the original Jewish followers of Jesus were thus totally superseded and were now heretical.

Those followers had included his mother, his brothers, and his closest companions. There had been no Virgin Birth in their teaching. The inauguration of the Messiahship of Jesus had taken place at his baptism by John the Baptist. According to the Jewish Christians the voice Jesus had heard as he rose from the water were those of *Psalm ii*: 'You are my son. *Today* I have begotten you.'

Accordingly in Mark's Gospel, reflecting the reminiscences of Peter, the story of Jesus in the capacity of Son of God begins with his baptism, not with his birth. Only from that moment was he 'the Anointed One' (the Messiah, Christ).

We have recognised that the Dear Disciple of the Fourth Gospel was not one of the Twelve. He does not appear to have been in the company of Jesus throughout his ministry; and his contribution, traditionally dictated in extreme old age at Ephesus, has something to tell us mainly of things not mentioned by the other Gospels, and which took place in Judea and Jerusalem rather than in Galilee. But some sixty years afterwards he could not have quoted verbatim the longish speeches of Jesus, and in any case we have given reason for attributing these to John the Elder who had never known Jesus. One of the things that tells against much in the Fourth Gospel is that throughout Jesus parades his Messiahship, which, if he had done so, would promptly have got him arrested. And the Synoptics make it very clear that it was not until almost the end of his ministry that Jesus admitted to being the Messiah.

Here the complete contradiction between the Fourth Gospel and the others is very significant. In the Fourth Gospel the Dear Disciple and Andrew are the first to acknowledge Jesus as Messiah, almost immediately after his baptism. And Andrew then reports this discovery to his brother Simon who was to be known as Peter. Almost immediately after Philip and Nathanael are convinced that Jesus is the Messiah.

In the other Gospels however there is no such discovery. The popular view of Jesus is that he is a prophet, perhaps Elijah, or even John the Baptist risen from the dead. Jesus never admits to being the Messiah; but towards the end of his activities he raises the matter of his identity with the Twelve. Peter blurts out then, 'You are the Messiah.' Jesus agrees but insists that the apostles keep this to themselves. The incident is followed immediately by the story of the Transfiguration, as a heavenly confirmation, attested by the Law (Moses) and the Prophets (Elijah).[2]

On every ground the Petrine representation is the more probable, and this has great significance. It means that since the Twelve for most of the ministry only thought of Jesus as a teacher and prophet there was no special reason for remembering very clearly what he had said and done and keeping a record. Of course, subsequently, incidents would be recalled, and tradition claims that after the death of Jesus an effort was made to compile recollections. Matthew, who was clearly literate because of his profession, had assembled a number of incidents and sayings utilised in the Gospels of *Matthew* and *Luke*, while Peter gave a number of addresses on his experiences with Jesus, of which Mark had taken notes.

But we must recognise that such primitive records as may once have existed were made subsequent to the lifetime of Jesus, and when he had positively been acknowledged as Messiah by a very substantial number of adherents. They included many erudite persons, priests, scribes and so on, Essenes and Pharisees, saturated in the Messianic interpretation of the Old Testament. The tendency would be for the recollections to be expended to magnify the personality of Jesus, especially to emphasise his identity as Messiah. Thus stress is laid on the significance of his baptism by John immediately followed by the Temptation in the Wilderness in his new capacity. The revelation of his Messiahship to the disciples at Caesarea Philippi is followed at once by the account of the Transfiguration of Jesus. Later, the evidences that he is the Messiah were shifted back from baptism to birth; and at the end of his career, prior to the Ascension, it is Jesus himself (according to *Luke*) who expounds to two of his followers the application to himself and his experiences of passages in all the Old Testament Scriptures. One of the earliest Christian documents was a collection of such quotations with their application.

Once there was a substantial body of erudite Jewish believers in Jesus as Messiah, testified to in the *Acts*, their concepts would rapidly make an impact on the Jesus story as related by those who had been close to him, yes, and even upon his mother and brothers. A blending would rapidly develop which conferred a new dignity on the close friends and family of the Messiah, so that they themselves would come to believe in the truth of much that was being advanced by Messianic exegesis and ingenuity.

With the creation of the Gospels, as we know them, in a Gentile environment outside the Holy Land, the tendency inevitably was to accommodate the Jesus story to circumstances beyond the Messianic.

This would be done in two ways, by the introduction where practicable of local colour in the narration of incidents and a slight movement into the environment of non-Jewish interpretation. Fortunately, because of the strength of tradition and the weight of Jewishness within Christianity this process could not be very extensive. Occasionally a point crops up in some manuscript reading or in a context that will allow of conveying the deity of Christ.

When Christianity became a fully developed religion in its own right, with an authoritative Creed, this last process would continue by one or two word changes and interpolations in certain manuscripts. It would also exhibit itself centuries ahead in certain translations into modern languages, with the simple device, for instance, of spelling Son of God with a capital S in relation to Jesus, but with a small s with reference to angels or to humans other than Christ.

For someone not an orthodox Christian those changes and intrusions are readily perceptible, and it is easy to make allowance for them. Unfortunately, to the contrary, it is not so easy for the Christian believer to perceive and comprehend the underlying Messianic representations, because their purport is not part of his equipment. We can already see the beginnings of the difficulties when someone like Paul had to try to communicate to Gentiles who Jesus was as Messiah (Christ), an idea almost completely alien to their notions; *christos* for Greek-speaking people simply meant something used as an ointment or salve.

With reasonable care and historical insight, and detachment from Christianity as a religion, it does not therefore lie outside the bounds of competence to discover a considerable amount about Jesus as he appeared to himself and to others. The first three Gospels in particular, because of their underlying sources and the conditions which gave rise to them, have preserved a great deal that is reliable and illuminating. For this we have to be deeply thankful. But we do have to probe with skill, and with knowledge of the circumstances of place and period. Necessarily, this must be more practicable for the Jewish scholar who is at the same time a Messianist.

The Messianic is a peculiarly Jewish ideology very hard for the non-Jew to comprehend. And if he does not comprehend it he cannot really understand the man who epitomised its significance, and to whom it meant everything. He has to start with the recognition of the topicality of the theme in the time of Jesus, when for multitudes of Jews the existing world order was about to terminate and the

Messianic Age (the Kingdom of God on earth) to be ushered in. Only such a conviction could have produced the spate of Essene prophetic literature spelling out the details. Only such a conviction could have produced the weird figure and message of John the Baptist. All the pious were alerted to study the Signs, both in the heavens and in the world. Labouring under the yoke of Rome multitudes of humble Jewish people were awaiting a word, a signal, an event, responding to inevitable charlatans and mentally deranged agitators. The pages of the Jewish historian Josephus are eloquent for anyone who genuinely seeks to imbibe the atmosphere of what we are pleased to call the first century AD.

And here was a boy, a scion of the House of David from which the Messiah was expected to come, a very sensitive, deeply impressionable boy, a pious and poetic boy, with doting parents contributing their support to his adolescent dream.

Everything was there, of faith, of feeling, of equipment, to respond to the impact of the contemporary obsession. The man of the Gospels is not someone vague, acting on impulse. He is a man ready, a man prepared, a man with a plan, which methodically he proceeds to put into action, as I sought to make clear in my bestselling book *The Passover Plot*. Jesus was no youngster when he put his programme into operation. The evidence points to his being in his thirties. And he was no fool. He was highly observant and analytical. He knew what he was up against in the rôle of Messiah – the authorities with their spies and informers, the oppressed Jewish populace eager to find a leader for revolt, pin-pricking pietists whose world was a chequer-board of do's and don'ts. And he knew much more – what the essence of the Messianic was.

NOTES AND REFERENCES

1. See Schonfield, *The History of Jewish Christianity.*
2. *Matthew* xvii.

134

19.

The Secret is out

The Messianic idea did not begin with a man, it began with a people. The vision looked back to the call of Abraham, to God's promise to him that in 'his seed' should all the nations of the world be blessed (*Gen.* xxii. 18). In a fashion of rabbinical exegesis Paul sought to convey that the term 'seed' meant One, namely the Messiah (Christ), in *Gal.* iii. But quite clearly in *Genesis* the term is collective, relating to Abraham's descendants. A nation is to be founded, not for its own glory and power but as a means of blessing all the nations of the earth.

Here is the golden thread that runs through the whole Bible. Israel's destiny is to be a Servant-Nation, a Priestly Nation, set apart from all the peoples of the world for this ministering function. 'Ye shall be unto Me a kingdom of priests, and a holy nation.' (*Exod.* xix.6) Thus in the end 'it shall come to pass that ten men out of all languages of the nations shall take hold of the robe of him that is a Jew, saying, "We will go with you; for we have heard that God is with you"' (*Zech.* viii. 20-23). As a consequence the nations will come to Zion to learn from the God of Israel, and there will be peace throughout the earth (*Isa.* ii. 1-4). As Jesus is said to have told the woman of Samaria, 'Salvation is of the Jews.' (*John* iv. 22)

In the book of the Prophet Isaiah (chs. xl-liii) we have the revelation of Israel as the Suffering Servant of God, the Messianic Servant-Nation. But it was no easy task for a nation to be set apart from all the others, to have a different function from all the others. Israel did not want this distinction, this mission, to labour and suffer on behalf of mankind. It did not want to be a Chosen People; it wanted to be like everyone else. The people came to the Prophet Samuel and told him, 'Make us a king to judge us like all the nations' (*I. Sam.* viii. 5).

Samuel warned them how kings in general treat their subjects. But the people would have none of it. 'Nay,' they cried, 'but we will have a king over us; that we also may be like all the nations, and that our king may judge us, and go out before us and fight our battles.' They were first given Saul.

Israel got its monarchy and lost its sense of mission. But the evil could still be turned to good. We learn of the anointing of the shepherd boy David, whose son would become God's son, Solomon (the Peaceable), and whose descendant as the anointed (christed) king of Israel would by his suffering and example lead his nation back to God, so that it would fulfil its mission of leading all the nations to God, and to His ways of peace and justice. We have to see the Bible story in its proper perspective. The Messianic mission to mankind is that of the nation to the nations. The personal Messiah is a secondary figure. He must save his nation, so that his nation may save the nations of mankind.

Jesus could qualify as the Messiah, adopted as Son of God in the character of king of the Jews, because he was descended from David. But so could others. What identified him in particular was that uniquely he had come to the knowledge of the Messiah's function in the regal capacity. It devolved upon him to lead his people back to its world mission.

Most earnestly from boyhood, as *Luke* conveys to us, Jesus sought to learn about the prophecies, what had been predicted of the function of the Messiah. In what have been called the Silent Years, in a period of Jewish history when the Messiah was being most anxiously awaited, Jesus realised what the true function of that personality was to be, as no one else did. It consorts very ill with the Church's doctrine that Jesus should have said, 'I am not sent but unto the lost sheep of the house of Israel,' (*Matt*. xv. 24), and that he told the Twelve (representative of the twelve tribes) not to go to the Gentiles, nor even the Samaritans (*Matt*. x. 5-6), only to Israel. Let the reader study again the Sermon on the Mount, for it is the epitome of the message of the king to his Jewish people.

And the climax of the story is fully in keeping. When Jesus knew that his call to his people to return to their mission was being largely unheeded it was then that he determined to shock them into repentance by suffering as king of the Jews on a heathen cross. He 'set his face steadfastly to go to Jerusalem' (*Luke* ix. 51). And there, just before the Passover, the festival of deliverance, he rode into his

136

capital as King Messiah to the plaudits of many, well knowing what the consequences would be.

Jesus was taken down from the cross on the same day as he was impaled on it, and his body came into the hands of his friends. Faith and legend have adorned the fact that two days later the tomb was found opened and empty. Whatever the reason, which is not too hard to seek, the Messiah henceforth could belong to the ages, the living symbol of a promise yet to be fulfilled, the witness to a Plan of God for our planet, when a nation will save the nations.

In the early teaching of the Messianic (Christian) as presented by Paul (*Rom.* xi; *Eph.* ii, etc.) the door was now open for individuals of all nations by faith in the King of Israel to cease to be Gentiles and become Israelites by adoption. Unfortunately the majority remained pagans at heart, and created a new religion with Jesus as the embodiment of its God. They began to persecute the Jews, and converted Jesus into the foe of Israel rather than its deliverer. The title Christ was preserved as a kind of surname of Jesus, and it is only in recent times – thanks to research and discovery – that the Messianic has begun to be comprehended in its real significance.

The day will come when Jesus will be given back to Israel, and Israel may then become the saviour of the nations, proclaiming to them, 'The Lord is *your* God, the Lord is One.'

Meanwhile we have the man, not a powerful and prominent man, but a rather puny man[1] of regal descent but artisan stock, a provincial man, who could identify himself in the most literal manner with the magic of the age-old Messianic Hope as now proclaimed and publicised by contemporary seers and interpreters of the Sacred Scriptures. What a challenge to which to respond! What a programme with which to be identified, to be involved in its details, to shape its fulfilment!

There was a glory in it, even a heady delusion of incarnating that imagined Heavenly Being, the Son of Man, whom the Essenes said was God's first creation; but also a humility, the humility of a very humble man, who would claim no eminence for personal power and prestige like the rulers of the Gentiles, only for the loving and dedicated service of God, the supreme Father.

The nearer inevitable death approached as a consequence of what had to be done, the more emphasis do we find of the faith of Jesus in 'the glory that should follow.' We may call such conviction a self-delusion, even a mania. The scenario was adorned with all the panoply of contemporary Jewish Messianic imagination; but it was very real for Jesus whose soul was saturated with such prophetic visions.

That faith was to make the frustrations, and the setbacks, and the inevitable horrors of the cross capable of being borne – though with a natural repugnance – by this highly sensitive personality. He reached out with his whole soul to God's fulfilment of the promises that in the coming Messianic Age would make the woes of the Messiah a sacrifice which Jesus could offer with sublime confidence, with fanatical assurance. That confidence, that certainty, is with us yet ringing down the centuries; and it is bound up uniquely and irrevocably with the extraordinary Hebrew imagination of a Messiah, a Christ, and what his mission would achieve for mankind.

NOTES AND REFERENCES

1. We have to visualise Jesus as slightly below average height, according to Christian tradition, and cf. *Luke* xix. 3.

Index